FROM BOTH SIDES OF THE
ATLANTIC

European relatives, their history and culture from which families
immigrated to North America with renewed hope for the future.

NORM ADOLPHSON

TRAFFORD
PUBLISHING™

Order this book online at www.trafford.com
or email orders@trafford.com

Most Trafford titles are also available at major online book retailers.

Printed in the United States of America.

ISBN: 978-1-4669-0016-5 (sc)
ISBN: 978-1-4669-0017-2 (e)

Trafford rev. 05/19/2012

 www.trafford.com

North America & international
toll-free: 1 888 232 4444 (USA & Canada)
phone: 250 383 6864 ♦ fax: 812 355 4082

Foreword

*We had a well-attended family reunion of the Adolphson family at the Valleyview Riverside Golf Course in July 2006. Stories were told of our parents and those who had passed away. I was asked if I would record some of the memories. As I started to do this, there was so much more to be recalled and recorded. I had two opportunities to visit Norway and one visit to Denmark and Germany. While over there, I was able to visit with and see the places where relatives and ancestors lived. With all this information, it seemed the right thing to share this and exchange our family stories. I believe it is important for our children to know about their "roots".

*It will be two years in April 2011, since I started gathering and writing and requesting stories from relatives and friends to submit their stories of their families. I wrote stories for some people and after they sent their own, I found there were duplications but I thought it best to leave it the way it was. Some of the events in the stories are remembered differently but I didn't change that either. It didn't matter much

*There were about 185 pictures sent to the publisher and if they turn out good it will be a good feature.

*The directory should create an incentive for contacting each other—especially for the Young people.

*This compilation of information grew way beyond what I first envisioned and I never considered myself and "author".

*It is difficult to do justice to everyone and I hope that if I made mistakes or did not mention something important, you will be forgiving.

*I hope you will enjoy this book

*   *   *

Norm Adolphson

Directory

Addresses by Family in Norway.

Alfred and Mina Odegaarten: Deceased

Ruth Drag-Nov. 14. 1929—Phone 011-47-32-82-24-71 cell-011-47-92-04-10 e-mail-re-wilhe@ online.no

Jonas Lies Vei 48

No-3022 Drammen Norway

Reiulf Wilhelmsen—Aug.22.1934—Information as above.—reiulf@reiulf.no

Children of Ruth Drag

Terje and Margrete Drag—Phone-011-47-23-25-15-45 e-mail-terje.drag@biware.no

Bjornerbben 43 A

No-0383 Oslo Norway

Children

Tore Drag—July 22,1992-Address as above

Hakkon Drag-July24,1992

Elsie Drag-Nov.8, 1995

Lauritz Arnold Emgaard was born to Anna Amundson who later married Alfred Odegaarten who raised him as well as thier daughters Eva and Ruth

Decendants of Lauritz Arnold and his wife Hedvig Kristine(Holstad)Emgaard deceased

Lauritz-Jan.l9,1913-July 16,1983

HedvigJune 3,1917-May19,1990

Anne Karine Sydtskow(Emgaard)-Feb.1, 1947-June2,2006

Sverre Sydskow(Emgaard)June 2 2006

Thale Annette Sydskow—Aug.13.1997—Cell-011-47-20-12-82—Email thel@dfs.no

Mads Sydskow Andresen July 5, 1970—Cell-01 1-47-91-19-60-60

Henrik Nygaard-Nov21 ,2000

Kaja Nygaard-Apri125,2005

Janicky Sydskow-Feb.28,1974—Cell-011-47-97-50-48-75

Siman Sydskow-Oct.10,2008

Magnus Sydskow-Oct.10,2008

Runar Emgaard DeclO.1958—Cell-011-47-97-55-70-54—Email-runar.emgaard@ebnett.no

Marcelina Emgaard Oct.5,1960—Cell-011-4792-25-31-51—Email—lina.emgaard@ebnet.no

Patrick Emgaard Dec.l 0, 1992—Cell-011-47-41-85-72-02—Email-patemgaard@hotmail.com

Eva Wilhelmsen and Erling deceased.

Erik&Elisabeth(Beber)Wilhelmsen—Cell-O11-47-41-50-85-92-Elisabeth   Cell-O11-47-40-[
n-3070 Sande—Email—erik.wilhelmsen@cavotec.com—Fax-011-47-41-60-85-

Norway—elisabeth-Email—elisabethheber@hotmail.com

Elizabeth's two daughters

Kristine—single

Cecile and Peder Nielsen 2 children— Sofie and Vetle

Erik's two daughters '

Sitone &Jarle Fotland—Email-sitonewilhelmsen@dnv.com—Phone-O11-47-95-23-36-82

—Email-jarle.fotland@dnv.com—Phone-011-47-99-03-89-98

Kristin and Kjetil—Email—Kristinwilhelmsen@dnv.com—Phone-O11-47-41-52-18-96 ~

Grandson of Tordis and Even Stenberg—Erik(Lauritz)Stenberg,father

Ruger &Lina Stenberg

Patrick Stenberg—Son

Ivar Berg—Email—ivberg@online.no—Phone—O11-47-33-77-64-47

Sandabuktveien 186—Cell—O11-47-40-46-62-96

N-3070Sande i Vestfold

Oscar &Ellen Adolphson Families

Norman & Yutta Adolphson—Email—normadolphson@yahoo.ca

P.O. Box 6,Valleyview,Ab—Phone—780 524 3667—Cell—780 524 7543

TOH3NO

3Daughters

Rhonda &Stan Reimer—Email—rhondareimer@shaw.ca

53 Lakeland Place—Phone—204 261 3736 home

Winnipeg, Man.—Phone—204 348 2541 cottage

R3C 4A8

2 granddaughters

Angela and Jonathan Klassen—Email—ang-reimer@hot.com

~-Lakeland place—Phone—204-293-6252~

539 Raglan Rd.

Winnipeg, Man. R3G 3E4

Amanda Reimer—Email—reimer-amanda@hotmail.com

53 Lakeland Place—Phone—204-960-7509

607 B Rathgar Ave.

Winnipeg,Man. R3L 1G5.*

Lorraine Claire—Email—lc1air@shaw.ca

60 Shoreline Circle—Phone—Cell—604 780 7829

Port Moody B.C.

daughter

Stefanie Broad—Email—autumn-falls/@hotmail.com

Address as above—Phone—604 562 4199

Sonia & Richard Ens—Email—damjos@hotmail.com

15222-104 Str.

Grande Prairie AB

T8X OJ5—Phone—780-533-2379

Joshua Ens—Email—joshua77@hotmail.com

15222-104 Str.

Grande Prairie AB

T8X OJ5—Phone—780-832-51 05

Damon Ens—Email—damon@9mail.com

15222-104Str.

Grande Prairie AB

T8X OJ5—Phone—780-533-2379—780-832-2275

Carissa Ens—Email—lid-2-board@hotmail.com

15222-104 Str.

Grande Prairie AB

T8X OJ5—Phone—780-533-2379—cell—780-533-2374

Arthur & May Joy Adolphson

Box 153

Valleyview AB

TOR 3NO—Phone—780-524-3738—cell—780-552-3736

Dean &Debbie Adolphson—Email—ddadolph@telusplanet.net

Box 573

Valleyview AB

TOR 3NO—Phone—780-524-4187—cell—780-524-9538

Marla & Gared Mayer—jarmay@telus.net

9602-86 Ave

Peace River AB

T8S lK4—Phone—780-624-9083—cell—780-701-9083

Sarah & Dale Hepfner—Email—sadolph@live.ca

RR I-Site 1 Box86

Morinville AB

T8R 1P4—Phone—780-70 1-9083

~ Dana Lea Adolphson

Box 573 Valleyview AB

TOH 3NO —Phone— 780-524 4187

Deanna Fitzmaurice—Email—deannafitz@shaw.ca

65 Ridgebrook Close

Sherwood Park AB

T8A 6L9—Phone—780-640-6517

4; Chelsea & Shawn Stepier—Email—che1seafitz@shaw.ca

1108-80 Str. SW

EdmontonAB

T6X 1E6—Phone—780-634-9133

Brittany Fitzmaurice—Email—britanyfitzmaurice@shaw.ca

14 Cypress Ave

Sherwood Park AB

T8A 114—Phone—780-441-1193

~Kathrine & John Mycek—Email—mycekfrm@telus.net

Box 327

DeboltAB

TOH 1BO—Phone—780-957-2677

. . . Keith & Helene Adolphson—Email—keith_al@telus.net—or—sprucehavenfarms@telus.net

Box 1864

Valleyview AB

TOH 3NO—Phone—cell-780-524-2902

Toni & Bob Romano—Email—allinthefamily77@shaw.ca

6935-21Ave

EdmontonAB

T6K 2H3—Phone—780-461-3456

Kaleb Romano—Email—same as above

6935—21 Ave

EdmontonAB

T6K 2H3—Phone—780-461-3456

Avery Romano—the same as above

Paige Ramano—same as above

Alice & Ken Hennig—Email—amahen711@shaw.ca

1253 Gilley Crescent

Parksville BC

V9T 1W5—Phone—25o-752-1932

Bonalin & Wayne Clearwater—Email—bonalin@shaw.ca

202-435 Morison, Ave.

Parksville BC

V9P 1W5—Phone—250-954-2135

Janet & Angus MacInnnes—Email—j anet_mac4ines@telus.net

405 Lakeside Green 780-458-0333

St. Albert AB

T8N 3T3—

Terry & April Bancesco—Email—boosteds@yahoo.com

16700 Ford Oaklane

Justin Texas

Phone— 817-710-60 18— cell —940-368-1357

Megan Bancesco—Email—mbancesco@gmail.com

Unit 3, 10032-113 Str

Edmonton AB—780-71 0-5440—Store—780-416-0438

Herman & Meta Pedersen Families.

Ellen Pedersen ,deceased, included in the Adolphson Family

George & Amy Pedersen,deceased,

Allan & Bette Pedersen—Email—boopboopdoop@shaw.ca

2146 Noel Ave

Comox BC

V9M 114—Phone—250-339-7179

(Richard Pedersen & Jennifer Bird—Email—abcbooks@shaw.ca

ABC Book Store

1950 Robb Ave

Comox BC

V9M 4C3—Phone—250-339-3334

Walter Pedersen

2146 Noel Ave

ComoxBC

V9M 114—250-339-7179

Melissa & James Black—Email—melisablack@shaw.ca

1276 Mckinley

Ladysmith BC

V9G 1R2—Phone—250-245-4822

—Bonnie & Harry Seutter—bseutter@rogers.com

51466 Range Road 232

Sherwood Park AB

T8B 1L1—Phone—house—780-467-0689—Golf Course—780-467-9254—cell—780-993-1125

Ryan & Alyson Seutter—ryanseutter@rogers.com

3514 McLay Crescent

EdmontonAB

T6R 3V3—Phone—780-435-7926

Jess & Christy Seutter—Email—jessandchristy@hotmail.com

51473 Range Road 232

Sherwood Park AB

T8B 1L1—Phone—780-449-6020

Bill & Viney Pedersen {deceased} Families

Ruth & Gordon Lennon—Email—grlennon@telus.net

197 Mount River Estates 403-249-5032

Calgary AB T3Z 3J3

Barbara & Gerry Nation—Email—bnation@mts.net—gnation@teus.net

Box 1853

Didsbury AB

TOM OWO—Phone—403-335-8054

Andrew Nation & Cheryl

Box 1022

Didsbury AB

TOM OWO—403-518-5470—403-355-8127

Hayden Bedford-Nation

Box 1853

Didsbury AB

TOM OWO—Phone—403-518-8054

Carmen Truong-Nation

Box 1853

Didsbury AB

TOM OWO—403-518-8054

Matthew Nation

Box 1853

Didsbury AB

TOM OWO—Phone—403-518-8054

Emily & Daniel Steffen—Email—rnilysteffen@hotmail.com

Box 2711

Didsbury AB

TOM OWO—Phone—403-439-0225

Grace Nation—Email—bnation@mts.net

Box 1853

Didsbury AB

TOM OWO—Phone—403-335-8054

Brenda & Harry Maekelburger—Email—hbmaekelburger@shaw.ca

127 Tuscany Hills Road NW

Calcary AB

T3L p,hone—403-547-6540

Trevor Maekelburger—Email—mba-Pro2000@hotrnail.com

127 Tuscany Hills Road

Calgary AB

T3L 1Z9—Phone—403-547-6540

Stephanie Maekelburger *—Email—step_on_me_mae@hotmail.com

127 Tuscany Hills Road

Calgary AB

T3Z lZ9—Phone—403-547-6540

-Christopher & Danielle Lennon—Email—chris@deerpark.ca

748 Crescent Road NW

Calgary AB

T2M 4A7—Phone—403-284-8054

—Don & Lois Pedersen—Email—Iois@albertahighspeed.net family

RR2 *V*

LacombeAB

T4L 2N2—.,—Phone—403-347-7560—cell—403-304-5589—office—403-347-3506

Debbra & Evert Weenink—Email—dweenk@xplanet.com

Bradley & Kelly Pedersen Email—bradp@tech4kids.com

455 Turnberry Crescent

Mississauga aNT

L4Z 1X8—Phone—905-507-0660—cell—41 7 356-2535

Bretton Pedersen—Email—kingbret@live.ca

455 Turnberry Crescent

Mississauga a Ontario

L4Z 1Z8—Phone—905-507-0660

Megan Pedersen—Email—megp77@live.com

455 Turnberry Crscent

Mississauga a Ontario

L4Z lZ8—Phone—905-507-0660

Rebecca & Darwin Carruthers—Email—carutr@xplanet.ca

RR2

LacombeAB

T4L 2N2—Phone—403-314-4459—cell—403-877-8918

~ Bruce Pedersen—Email—pedersen@northwestel.net

41 Iron Horse Drive

Whitehorse Yukon

YIA 6T4—Phone—867-633-8492—867-633-5241

Susan Pedersen—Email—susanped@gmail.com

25 Baile Close

Red Deer AB

Jodi Lyn & Kenton Poelzer *—Email—kpoelzer@hotmail.com

443 Barret Drive

Red Deer AB

T4R IM2—Phone—403-348-2007

Jonathan & Tamara Pedersen *—Email—jonpeder@hotmail.com

5817-56 Ave.

Red Deer AB

T4R 3A3—phone—314-1319

Tami Pedersen *—Email—tami.pedersen@signalta.com

101 1414—12 Str.SW

Calgary AB

T3C 3T2—Phone—403-698-4303

Sheri Pedersen *—Email—pedersen@northwestel.net

41 Iron Horse Drive

Whithorse Yukon

YIA6T4

David & Emily Pedersen *

41 Iron horse Drive

Whithorse Yukon temporary address

Y1A 6T4—Phone—cell—403-200-7585

Bryan & Denise Pedersen—Email—bryan—Pedersen@decnet.com

1616 Grandeview Rd

Gibsons BC

VON 1V5-~—phone~—604-886-8660

Daniel Bruce & Sarah Alison (Fisher}Pedersen *—Email—dbpedersen@shaw.ca

170-101 Parkside Drive

Port Moody BC

V3H 4W6—Phone—778-838-5387—778-837-9829

Michaela Lyn & Doren Jen Aldana *—Email—michaela.aldana@gmail.com

3608 Deercrest Drive # 503

North Vancouver BC

V7G 2S8—Phone—604-683-4411—604-990-4303

Michael Donald @ Ruth Pedersen *—Email—mdpedersen@shaw.ca

3132 River Rd.

Port Coquitlam BC

V3C 1R4—Phone—604-317-7678

—Ann & Lome Wedlund—Email—Iawedlund@hotmail.com box 5664 ~

LacombeAB

T4L lX3—403-782-2571

Laura & Darren Carlson *—Email—carlson@albertahighspeed.net

RR3 Lacombe AB

T4L 2N3—Phone—403-782-5256

Darren & Myra Wedlund *—Email—Box

5971

LacombeAB

T4L 1X3—Phone—403-348-9721

Krista & Marshel Harrod *—Email—mkharrod@planet.com

Box 6017

LacombeAB

T4L 1X5—Phone—403-506-9472

Angela Wedlund *—Email—angwedlund@hotmail.com

Box 5664

LacombeAB

T4L 1X3—403-782-2571

Arthur & Maryanne Pedersen (deceased) Families

—Morris & Hazel Pedersen *—Email—mhpedersen@shaw.ca

Box 2874

Blackfalds AB

TOM OJO—Phone—403-600-0700—cell—403-506-1854

Robin & Kathy Pedersen

LacombeAB

Lavonne & Gordon Sylvester no information available

Janelle & Corey Johnson

Regina SASK.-no other information available

Mabel & Roy Schmidt-*—Email—royschmidt@shaw.ca

#307 5300-48 Str.

Red Deer AB

T4N 7C5—Phone—403-347-7367 ,

Greg Lytle

Box 3246

Spruce Grove AB

Brian Lytle—Email—blytle68@gmail.com

RR4

Innesfail AB

P4G IF9—Phone—403-227-0052—cell—403-505-0432

James & Marilyn Pedersen *—Email—pastorjm6@shaw.ca

16113-88a Ave

EdmontonAB

T5R 4N5—Phone—780-757-8000

Timothy & Missy Pedersen—Email—timp3068

620 Desertfield Drive

Palms Springs California

92264—Phone—760-323-5207

Christy & Todd Shentaler—Email—here2stay@shaw.ca

120 Sandstone Estates

Stoney Plain AB

T7Z OE2—Phone—780-963-1454

Daniel & Tami Pedersen—Email—bspedersen@mac.com

511 North Elm Ave

Hastings Nebraska 68902—Phone—402-834-0238

Mark & Kendra Pedersen—Email—mpedersen@hotmail.com

5650 Windsor Way 303

Culvor City

California 90230—Phone—31 0-686-3971

David Pedersen

#933133 Bourquin Cresc.

Abbotsford BC

V2S 6B1—Phone—604-852-1426—cell—604-302-1499

Wayne & Jean Pedersen *—Email—wpedersen7@shaw.cal

47 Wyndham Crescent Y

Red Deer AB

T4N 7G9—Phone—403-314-5448

Jonathan & Steffanie Pedersen—Email—oatmeal@hotmail.com

Calgary AB—403-698-1803

Melody Pedersen

No information available

Karen & Mark Stetson—Email—oatmea1@hotmail.com

Svend Julius @ Eva Pedersen (youngest brother of Herman Pedersen

—Anne1ise & Erik Tjustrup *—email—annelise@tiustrup.dk

Havretofen 16-Dk 2800 Kgs.

Lyngby Denmark—Phone—011-45-45-88-37-44 l' Karen Tjustrup—Email—karen.tjustrup@hotmail.com

Fuglsangpark 184 Dk-3520

Farum Denmark—Phone—O11-45-44-99-66-08

Lone Tjustrup 01ufsen—Emai1—1one@olufsen.dk

Ronnebaervej 119 DK-2840

Holte denmark—Phone—011-45-45-46-13-31

Holger Madsen,Frind of the Family

His relatives:

Henning & Anna Christiansen—Email—hchristiansen@mail.dk

Praestegardsvj 59

Ingstrup 9480

Lokken Denmark—Phone—011-45-98-88-34-37

,Jakob Christiansen *—Email—jakob.chr@gmail.com

20 3TV-800 Arhus C

Ringkokobingvej Denmark—Phone—O11-45-40-44-38-19

Ida Christiansen *—Email—udichri@hotmail.com

855-Risskov

Bakketoften Denmark—Phone—O11-45-61-78-91-18

Wilhelm (Bill) & Madeline Klumbies Family

Kurt & Helma Klumbies *

478-Burrows Crescent Edmonton AB

T6R 2L3—Phone—780-434-0913

Diane & Ron Hinz—Email—rhinz@telusp1anet.net

499-523-28 RR 233

Sherwood Park AB

T8B OA2—Phone—780-464-5328

Hinz Children

Leanne & Kaylan Austing—Email—austings@shaw.ca

400 nottingham Blvd

Sherwood Park AB

T8A 5Z4—Phone—780-464-6481

Jennifer & Daniel Engelman—Email—daniel@engelman.ca

9736-78 Ave

Edmonton AB—Phone—780-249-5S68

Candice Hinz—rhinz@telusplanet.net

499-523-28 RR 233

Sherwood Park AB

T8B OA2—Phone—780-464-S328

—Brenda & Rudy Streu—Email—bstreu@gmail.com

301S-Wales Road

Kelowna BC

VIZ 2A7—Phone—*250-769-8016*

Streu Children

Amanda **Streu**—Email—amanda.streu@gmail.com

301S-Wales Road

Kelowna BC

VIZ 2A7—Phone—*250-769-8016*

Kelsey Streu—Email—kelseystreu@hotmail.com

301S-Wales Road

Kelowna BC

VIZ2A7

Sharon & Alvin Thomas—Email—maxxy@Shaw.ca

4 Edwin Crescent

St.Albert AB

T8N 7G9—Phone—780-569-5328

Oscar Adolphson 1892-1965

Dad

Our Dad

*Our father, Oscar Adolphson was born on November 15, 1894, in Sande, Norway. He was the third eldest child. The children were Alfred, Tordis, Anna (who died at the age of four). Dad and Andrew (who was 14 years younger than Dad).

*Sande is a village about a half-hour's drive from Drammen, where Dad attended school until Grade 8, We saw and took pictures of this school. He was quite good in school as he was in a special class with two other students and had gained a year. He had the same male teacher for the eight years he attended school.

*When Dad was 14 years old, he got a job at a local bank where he recorded and ran errands—there were no telephones at that time. He also worked with our grandfather, who was a butcher, going from farm to farm butchering animals, cutting and curing the meat and making sausage. Dad became very proficient at this because of the little tricks he had learned from his father.

*Our father was an accomplished ski jumper and would take part in competitions in the area. The Norwegian ski jumping championships were held in Oslo and still are to this day. The ski jump is called Holmenkollen and he attended this event as a spectator. The King of Norway took part at that time. We went up near the top of the jump, first by elevator and then by stairs. What a view! The bowl down below looked so small. It would take a lot of nerve to ski down that trestle!

*Our grandfather Adolf chose the last name for his children to be Odegaarten.

It was a common practice at that time to take the father's first name, adding sen for son or datter for daughter. For example, Adolph's family would be Adolphsen or Adolphdatter. Our name was Anglicized so that f in Adolphsen became ph and sen became son. Our grandfather opted for calling his daughters Odegaarten. It seemed that it was preferable at that time. There was also a practice of using the name of the farm you lived on as the family name. Uncle Alfred's middle was Adolfsen. This is the name he used when he arrived in the United States about five years before our Dad arrived. Our Dad chose this name as well, but it was changed to Adolphson.

*Besides being a butcher by trade, our grandfather Adolph Teodor Andreassen Odegaarten, according to Dad and Uncle Andrew, was a lay minister and led a group of Baptist believers who met in various homes.

Our grandfather also loved to fish. He owned a small sailboat that he could also row. He would take Dad fishing with him, and Dad really enjoyed that. *When Dad decided to go to the U. S., he told his father that he would stay there for three years and earn enough money to purchase a larger fishing boat. His plan was to return to Norway and go into the fishing business together with his father. But this plan never came to be.

*Dad was 16 when he left Norway in 1912, and he never saw his parents or sister again. On the morning dad left for the U. S., his father made him breakfast and saw him off on the local train. His mother was so grief-stricken that she could not get out of bed to see him on his way.

*Uncle Alfred had already been in the U.S. for four or five years by that time, so he paid for Dad's passage over, a debt that Dad later repaid.

*Dad landed in the U. S. with a cousin from the father's side of the family, Andrew Shervik. They met up with Uncle Alfred for a day or two but they all had jobs to go to so they parted for a few months until Uncle Alfred and Dad were able to meet again. Uncle Alfred planned to return to Norway for their parents' twenty-fifth wedding anniversary, and while he was in Norway, he got married.

As his new wife was not interested in moving to the U. S., Uncle Alfred never returned to North America to work. In 1964, he came to Canada to visit his brothers and their families.

*Uncle Alfred got a job doing construction for the railway not too long after returning to Norway from the U. S. He continued to work there in various capacities until he retired. At the end of his career, he was working as a conductor. This entitled him to a railway pass throughout most of Europe—which he used.

*Mom and Dad had arranged for a visit to Norway the following year but Dad died before this would take place.

*Much the same happened to our grandfather, Adolph. He immigrated to the U.S. sometime between 1881 and 1884 and worked for a large grain farmer (Dahlremple) until he returned to Norway. He also married his girlfriend in Norway, who refused to immigrate to the U.S. Because our great-grandfather regretted being unable to stay in the U.S, he encouraged Uncle Alfred to go.

Alfred went to work for Mr. Dahlremple for a while. When our Dad came over, he also worked for the same grain farmer. Dad often mentioned the great number of horses that were on the farm. He had opportunity to run a grain binder along with several other horse-drawn binders. This was his first exposure to grain and livestock farming, which he greatly enjoyed.

*Dad helped build a concrete dock on a small lake close to the main house, Dad also worked in a logging camp. He did not know a word of English. A North American Indian befriended him. The two would find a quiet place and open the Sears-Roebuck catalog. The Indian would point to a picture and ask what it was in Norwegian and then he would laugh.

*Dad had worked for a small wagon factory where he learned some blacksmith and wheelwright skills. This knowledge was helpful for the farming that would be in his future. I remember Dad's building a circular fire to heat a steel tire for a wagon when I was a small boy. Both of us used tongs to quickly lift the rim and place it on a wooden-spoke wheel. The wood squeaked and smoked as the rim contracted around the wheel.

*Dad did buy a small farm in Campia, Wisconsin, which is near; Rice Lake, a short distance east of Minneapolis.

*When we visited that area in 1972, we met two Engness families and all the relatives on our grandfather's side of the family in the U.S. We also met a single man named Shervik, who was related to Dad's cousins Andre and Hilmar Shervik. Mr. Shervik showed us a barn that had been damaged by tornadoes in the early1900, which was rebuilt twice and is still standing.

*Dad also had a bachelor uncle by the name of Martin Anderson, who was his Grandfather's brother. Dad, Mom and Janet visited the area two or three years prior to Dad's death.

*The newly married Bjorn and Elizabeth Engness were visiting the Engness families in Rice Lake when we were there in 1972. Bjorn worked for SAS Airlines in Oslo as an airplane mechanic. We were unable to locate this family when we visited Norway. It is a possibility that he could have been transferred to Copenhagen.

*Hilmar Shervik moved back to Norway in 1922 and bought a farm near Sande. He is buried there. I have pictures of that farm and his grave stone.

Dad stayed with his Uncle Martin Anderson on occasion. As Dad was only 17 years old, he could not get a mortgage on his own. Uncle Martin co-signed for him so he could buy a nearby farm. When we were visiting, we took photographs of a shed that our Dad had built on the farm, Uncle Martin Anderson's grave and a Lutheran church that our Dad and other relatives had attended. Adolph Engness' brother and wife owned the farm when we were there. Adolph and his wife, kathryn visited us in Valleyview, Alberta.

*The farm that Dad bought was a logged-out timber berth with a few open acres. It was rocky and had huge stumps that had to be removed with dynamite. After being there for a while, he decided there was not much future in the farm, so he began to search for other opportunities. While working for the American Bridge Company in Duluth, Minnesota, he joined the Sons of Norway. (He met Carl Svensen there, of whom I will write later.) The Sons of Norway had articles and ads about homesteads that could be bought for five dollars per quarter section. Uncultivated land in the Peace River country was available from the Alberta Government. The same was true in Argentina, except the land offered there was available by the square mile. After considering his options, Dad could not decide on which country to pick so he flipped a coin. He then headed to the Peace River country! As World War 1 ended in 1918, Dad was free to quit his job on the ore dock on Lake Superior. It had been classified as an "essential project" because of the American involvement in the war. Dad then headed north to Canada.

*Dad arrived in Grande Prairie in the spring of 1918, applied for and acquired the southwest quarter of 22-70-22-W5, where part of the town of Valleyview is presently located. This area was just opening up so there were very few homesteads at the time. Only one family, the Wallers, lived nearby.

*There were huge timber stands in Valleyview and the surrounding area. There was so much timber, in fact, that it had little value. Fire had passed through before Dad had arrived, but it stopped just short of where the present Hillside High School in Valleyview is located. The timber extended through the east end of town down to the Little Smoky River. Another fire burned off the rest of the timber just before 1928 when the major influx of homesteaders arrived. There were terrible fires that burned the surrounding area through the 1930s to mid-1950s. The smoke would sometimes make your eyes tear and the ash would fall in the perfect form of evergreen needles.

*Dad built a small log house and spent time until 1922 clearing and breaking his land during the summer. He had formed a partnership with three other carpenters, who contracted their labor to construct buildings in Grande Prairie,. In 1922, he bought cattle and moved them to the homestead permanently to begin ranching.

*For the first ten years, Dad lived on the homestead. He got his mail and groceries at Sturgeon Lake. In winter, he brought his main provisions such as 100-pound sacks of flour and sugar, jam, lard, kerosene and other supplies from Grande Prairie. It was a larger center and the trail there was much better than to High Prairie.

*Around 1927, Dad decided he would go to Saskatchewan and visit two cousins who were farming there. He mentioned that they had a bumper crop and had to use their living room to store grain. While visiting there, he again met Carl Svensen, who, due to health reasons, was looking for land in a dryer climate. Dad invited him to come to Valleyview. Carl arrived in 1928 and homesteaded the quarter of land that lies to the present southwest of 50 Avenue and 50 Street. This was quite coincidental! As mentioned earlier, they had met at a social club in Duluth, Minnesota.

*Because Carl and Dad had barns, they became stoping places for travelers on the new road through the community.

*In 1928 or earlier, two Swedish Lutheran Ministers, who were visiting the area, asked Dad if they could use him as a contact person to whom they could send prospective homesteaders.

*When the rush of homesteaders came to the area in 1928, many of them had been corresponding with Dad. When they arrived, he took them through the area to choose their homesteads. As it turned out, some did not follow through in "proving" their homesteads.

*The area of Valleyview was originally known as Red Willow—a name given to it by the Natives. In 1929 or 1930 a post office was established. The name Red Willow was already taken by a community near Stettler, Alberta, so a new name was required. This came about when the

Harrington brothers in Sturgeon Heights sent a package to Dad addressed to the "Valleyview Ranch". As this was quite descriptive of the area, Dad suggested that the name Valleyview be used for the name of the new post office, and the postal Department accepted this suggestion.

*As there were now a number of young families in the area at the time, there was need of a school, so a log schoolhouse was built by local homesteaders. It was located one and three-quarter miles Northwest of Valleyview's present 50 Avenue and 50 Street. It was not insulated so the heat from the stove, which was located in the back of the room, quickly dissipated. But at the front of the room, the teacher had to keep on her outdoor clothing. Lunches that had frozen on the way to school in the morning were put under the stove to thaw in time for lunch. The school also served as a community hall and church.

*As Dad was a carpenter by trade, he built many log homes and hip-roofed barns for homesteaders in the area.

*In 1931 our Mother, Ellen Pedersen, came to Valleyview to teach in this schoolhouse. Our parents met and our Dad took our Mother on their first date. He picked her up in a horse-drawn stone boat with two chairs placed side-by-side. This did not discourage our Mother though . . . they were married July 19, 1934.

*Mom traveled to High Prairie, the nearest hospital, two to three weeks before I, Norman, was to enter the world, which was July 1, 1935. As the roads were wet and muddy, Dad rode the saddle horse, Chubby, to visit Mom and me for a few days. There he met Paul Werklund. Paul invited Dad to ride home to Valleyview with him in his truck. Dad threw the saddle in the truck box and sent Chubby off home with a light slap on the hind quarter. Before Dad arrived home, Chubby was already there, having jumped into the pasture to join the other horses.

*Starting with a Model A Ford, Dad started a trucking service that spanned from 1936 to 1945. In 1938, he bought a one and a half-ton Chevrolet and in 1940 he purchased a new Chevrolet Maple Leaf three-ton truck. Dad hauled grain and livestock for the local farmers and mail and freight for the local stores. Around 1943 or 1944, Dad also hauled telegraph poles for the United States Army between High Prairie and the Big Smoky River. During this time, he also had a British American Oil dealership, selling gasoline by the 45-gallon barrel. On top of the telegraph poles, he also transported mail and supplies for local stores, as well as barrels of gasoline.

*Arthur was born March 17, 1938, at home. This was not planned—he arrived too soon! This is the first event that I remember. There were unusual things going on and I did not like it. I also remembered Dad showing my little brother to me, and he was in my crib!

*On November 7, 1942, the first girl of the family, Alice, was born in the High Prairie Hospital. She was strong and robust, could hold her own and was quite an athlete. She was the only one who learned to play the piano.

*Janet arrived on July 31, 1952, at the Grande Prairie Hospital. She was a welcome surprise to us all.

*In 1955 Dad acquired the John Deere Dealership for the Valleyview area. Art and I helped build the shop for the business, which Dad operated until the end of 1957. During this time, I was renting the farm but helping Dad run the business by doing all the ordering, letter writing and helping with the assembly of machinery—when I had time.

*In 1958, we switched roles and I ran the dealership for three years while Dad returned to farming until he and Mom retired in the farmhouse in town.

*That same year, Dad decided to move to the Little Smoky River to build a new farmstead. Our well had dried up in town and could not support the cattle that he wanted to keep. Instead he wanted to move the farm to a more reliable source of water. He built a house and moved the barn, garage and a couple sheds and some fencing from the farm site in town. I thought he should sell the cattle and retire in town, and I am sure that Art and Alice felt it was too much work to take on, but Mom thought it was a great idea because she wanted to move out of town.

*Dad liked to entertain little kids by taking them on his knee and singing, "Reada, Reada, Runka, Hesten Vota Plunka." Then he would take their little hands and recite a Norwegian poem by first pointing to their thumb and saying, "tumerstuton" and moving down through the fingers, reciting, "slykapotten, longamun, lyasven and Little Penny Jensen."

*When Janet was three or four years old, he would read Winnie the Pooh to her. The rest of the family enjoyed this also, especially because of his Norwegian accent, which made the story even funnier.

Another funny incident happened as a result of Dad's patching a truck tube in the kitchen one winter. He pumped it full of air to make sure it didn't leak after repairing it. Later that evening he went out to play cards with the "boys" when time got away on him. He got home about 4:00 a.m. and quietly snuck through the dark kitchen of the old farmhouse. He didn't want to wake Mom, but as he skulked around, he stepped on the tube and the strange squeak scared him. It scared him so badly that he jumped onto the now-cold kitchen stove. He sure felt foolish when Mom met him in the kitchen with her flashlight.

*Three months after suffering a stroke, Dad passed away on June 7, 1965.

*Dad had been active on school boards. He served on the local school board. Later in about 1943 he served on the founding school board of East Smoky School Division #54. He also served in the early 1950s for a total of seven years.

*When the primary school was built, the school board advertised for name suggestions to be submitted. Bonalin Hennig suggested "Oscar Adolphson Primary School". I was on the school board at the time and excused myself from the vote so there would be no conflict of interest issues. The name was accepted.

Ellen Adolphson—1910-2001

Mom

Our Mom

*Herman and Meta Pedersen grew up in Denmark, eloped to Iceland and later moved to Fredericia, Denmark, where Herman's father owned a successful tailor shop. There he worked for his father and learned the tailoring trade. Uncle George also learned this trade from his father in the same shop. There were tailors in the family for 5 generations.

*Ellen, our Mom, was born in 1910 and over the next ten years four boys were added to the family—George, Bill, Art and Ed.

*Our grandfather had itchy feet. He went overseas to Camrose, Alberta, and started his own tailor shop there. Mom was about nine years old at the time. She had to learn a new language but coped very well in school.

*Our grandfather then decided to go to Davenport, Iowa, to train for the chiropractic profession. After he graduated, he spent some time in Mexia, Texas which is just south of Dallas. Later he moved his family back to Denmark and practiced chiropractic there for a short time. Subsequently, he moved back to Camrose to start a practice. The family moved with him, and the children were continually changing schools. With all these moves, Mom managed to keep up her grades and graduated as a teacher from Camrose Normal School.

*Grandfather began to do well financially and bought a new Model T Ford with a canvas top. The family decided to visit some friends in the country. While having coffee, they looked out the window to see that their friends' goat had jumped onto the Model T. All four feet had gone through the roof and the goat was suspended by it's belly. This was probably hard on their friendship!

*After graduating from Normal School in 1931, Mom came to Valleyview to teach in the old log school that I attended and which I mentioned earlier. Then she continued teaching in other areas of the province near Camrose until 1934 when our parents married.

*Our grandmother, Meta, had returned to Denmark in 1932. She was apparently tired of all the moving and the hard times she had endured, especially as a mother of a large family.

*Our grandfather attended Mom and Dad's wedding in Edmonton,

Alberta, on July 19, 1934. Shortly after the wedding, he concluded his business in Camrose and returned to Denmark as well. He had arranged temporary housing for the two youngest children. Art and Ed were supposed to go back to Denmark within a few months, but they both decided against it. None of the children ever saw their father again as he died of cancer at an early age in Denmark around 1943. They were about 14 and 16 years old.

*Ed came to stay with Mom and Dad and attended school in Valleyview. He was 14 years old when he arrived, and left to go on his own when he was

20. To me, Ed was like and older brother. He always had a special place in our family, and Mom and Dad were like his own parents.

*Uncle Bill and Uncle Art lived together in Camrose where they started a garage business.

*Grandmother Meta came to visit us in Canada for about six weeks in 1946. She died of cancer the following year.

*Our Mother's parents became involved in a Plymouth Brethren work in Denmark and when they moved to Canada, the family joined a Baptist church.

Our grandfather sometimes taught Sunday School. He was a gifted story teller and could be very humorous.

*Our grandfather and grandmother were buried in a Lutheran cemetery in Fredericia, Denmark. Their graves were removed just before we visited Denmark because the lease had not been renewed. Land is very scarce so this is a common occurrence in some European countries. We have pictures of the graveyards in both Denmark and Norway.

*Mom had some interesting accomplishments in life, such as being an excellent swimmer. She and several other girls swam to islands surrounding Denmark, this was a concern for the Danish Coast guard. At a very young age, she learned to play a handcrafted violin, which was a high-quality instrument. Bonalin has the violin now and is planning to learn how to play it. Mom also learned to play piano. Rhonda received the piano from Grandma and has since refinished it. Tradition continues as her daughter, Angela, has become an accomplished pianist and will inherit the piano.

*Mom adapted to farm life. She grew a large garden, and she canned beef, pork, chicken, fish, vegetables and wild meat. Mom and Dad were married in the middle of the Depression (July 1934) so money was not plentiful. She knitted socks and mittens from raw wool that she carded. She also made blankets for the family. One of her creations was shoes for Art and me—these were made out of mackinaw coats and the soles from the backs of worn-out leather mitts. Art and I had homemade mattresses that were stuffed with straw. As Dad was in the trucking business, Mom did the outside chores such as feeding and watering the pigs and milking the cows.

*Some might think we were poor and neglected, but we were well-fed, clothed and looked after by our parents. Quite possibly, we even had a better family life because we had to be in the same room fairly close to the wood heater and kerosene lamp; so we had interaction with our parents and our siblings, which is sometimes not as easy today.

*While Dad was hauling groceries, we would get some items that were hard to acquire, such as sugar, bananas, coffee, candy and chocolate bars—but not very often. There were two general stores in town and a Hudson's Bay store at Sturgeon Lake. Being a freighter, our Dad would buy flour and sugar in 100-pound bags—usually from High Prairie in later years.

*From 1942 to 1943, Valleyview was without a teacher, so Mom taught me grade two by correspondence, which was a lot of extra work for her. She began teaching again from 1960 to 1980. She taught several of her grand-children—Dean, Deanna, Kathy, Keith, Rhonda, Lorraine, Sonia, Blaine and Bonalin.

*Mom was an avid reader with good retention. She was a committed Christian who studied the Bible and Bible-related literature as well as other areas of interest.

*After Dad died in 1965, Mom obtained her driver's license and continued to drive into her early eighties. She had two successful hip operations, one at age 77 and the other when she was 85 years old. She could stand and tie her shoes right until the end of her life.

*Mom moved into the Red Willow Lodge for her final three to four years of her life. She lived with relatively good health until her death at 90 years of age.

Andrew (Anders Adolphson)

*As mentioned earlier, Andrew was the youngest in Dad's family. When Andrew was four or five his parents took in his nephew Erik (Lauritz) Sternberg.

Erik was the oldest child of Tordi's 12 children. Andrew taught him to swim.

Erik could swim on his back and play the mouth organ at the same time. I met Erik's son, wife and 12 year old son in 2007.

*Andrew did a lot of the housework when our grandmother got sick with diabetes. She died in her early sixties. We have many pictures of our Norwegian relatives, their home, schools and tombstones.

*There was a pulp mill built across the fjord from where Andrew's family lived. There was also a hydroelectric plant built on a mountain stream, located about six-to-eight miles from where they lived. They were all able to have electricity in the 1920s. These are no longer in existence.

*Our great-grandfather died when our grandfather was 12 years old. A relative, Ole Boggan, was appointed as trustee to look after grandfather's inheritance, which was land covered with mature timber. Once the pulp mill started up, the timber became valuable. Somehow, Ole swindled our grandfather out of the timber berth. Ole developed this timber berth by making ice chutes down the mountainside so the logs would go at high speed down these troughs and shoot out into the deep water and not be damaged. While Andrew was still living in Norway, things were going well for Ole Boggan, so he bought a new Model T Ford. One day he went to town and parked in front of the local store. He had to stand in front of the car and use a hand crank to start the engine. He had left it in gear, and when he started it, it lurched forward, pinning Ole to the store and killing him. Andrew told me the story several times and he would always wind it up by swinging his fist through the air with an expletive indicating, "That was good for that S.O.B.!"

*Andrew had worked part-time loading ships at that same pulp mill.

*After Andrew had finished school, he and a cousin worked on a ship, hauling freight from Germany to Melbourne, Australia. They sailed through the Mediterranean Sea and the Suez Canal. He saw Mount Sinai where Moses had been given the Ten Commandments. Coming back from Australia, they followed the west coast of Africa back to Norway, Andrew's cousin was a cook on the ship and Andrew worked as the cook's helper.

*Work was hard to find. As Andrew didn't want to go back on the ship again, he did odd jobs including working as a gardener.

*Andrew decided he would immigrate to Canada so he wrote to Dad, asking him for a loan for the ticket. When Andrew immigrated to Canada in 1929, he was 21 years old. Arriving in Halifax, the immigration station looked like a cattle yard. (We saw it and took pictures). He didn't like Canada very much at first and wanted to return to Norway, but the Depression had set in and travel was not possible. Andrew took a homestead across the Little Smoky River from where we lived. He never did go back to Norway to visit and by the time he could afford to move back to Norway, he decided he liked it better here. About three years ago, I got an aerial picture of his farmstead taken in the 1950s. It was very neat and tidy, which was normal for Andrew.

*We would go to Andrew's place and stay for a week or two when Art and

I were young boys. When I was about eight years old, Andrew would have me drive the horses with the hayrack and tramp the hay down as it was being hand-loaded. This was hard work for a little kid! For dessert each day, I had to pick wild strawberries and raspberries on the hay field. The strawberries were huge and when served with cream and sugar tasted so good. Andrew also baked excellent bread and buns.

*When Andrew wanted to sell his farm, I purchased it. We moved his house across the river on the ice and put it in our farmyard for Andrew to live in. I hired him to help me on the farm doing cattle chores in winter and driving tractors on a part-time basis. This worked out well for all concerned. Sometimes he worked with our girls and they got along well.

*Always remaining a bachelor, Andrew retired at about 65 years of age. Eventually he moved to the Red Willow Lodge when he was about 78 years old. He enjoyed his stay at the lodge and enjoyed getting visitors. He lived there until he died suddenly in 1992 at the age of 84.

The building in the background survived the fire of 1900's and is presumed to be part of the original set of buildings from the 1500's

Hauling manure on a farm that dates back to 1500 AD in which we can trace our ancestry Erik Wilhelman and Ivor Berg talking with owner of the farm

3 point hitch on front end 6410. Barn and feeder cattle in back ground

These are 2 pictures of our grandfather's house that he built when Uncle Andrew was still at home. He rented out space to tourists. The depression of the 1930's came along and he disposed of it. It is located about 1/4 mile from Uncle Alfred's cabin

This picture is taken of grandfathers house from the south-east not far from Holm which was a small railway station that was located from where our father would have walked to when he left for the States—probably 1/2" of a km. the railway is still there but the station is gone

This is the last home our grandparents lived in after our grandmother died, our grandfather moved after sometime and lived in Uncle Alfred's cabin a short distance away where he died while talking to a neighbor. This house was modernized shortly before these pictures were taken

Anna and Alfred Odegaarten

Adolf T.A Odegaarten

Tordis Stenberg

Andrew and Oscar Adolphson

Adolf's children are Alfred, Tordis, Oscar and Andrew

This picture shows the side of Ruth's cabin Uncle Alfred's cabin in the background as well as Erik's cabin to the right.?? Erik standing is Uncle Alfred's stepson who is dead. Grandmas who he raised who is dead

As can be seen the house is about as close to the sea as you can get
The house has been modernized since we were there in 1989. We have pictures of it that year our great grandfather Odegarten's last home.

Uncle Alfreds cabin from the front with the deck added

Picture of Uncle Alfreds cabin from the back overlooking the fjord. Uncle Alfred landscaped the side hill with flat stones that we right at hand

Walkin basement storage in cabin, there were a few carpenter tools of our grandfathers stored

Ruth and her former husband used to own this cabin. It is directly in front of Uncle Alfred's cabin part of which can be seen at the back

View of Ruth and Reiulf's cabin on fjord

Andrew Sharvik's farm. I believe this is where Uncle Andrew fell from this ramp and bridge inside the barn right to the main floor. They were just about to bring in the first load of hay and several small kids were playing on it

He was bed ridden for several weeks and never saw a doctor

Old railway station which has been converted to a cafe the tracks were moved out of town—this is the town of Sande where our dad went to school near his home. Rieulf looking on

Same church in Sande. Our grandparents were buried here. Their graves were removed and six soldiers are buried there after they crashed. They were from the Australian Air Force

Hilmer Skjaivik—cousin of dad's who was in the U.S. with him and returned to Norway about 1920

View of the valley and fjord from Ruth's house of the city of Drammen

Ruth Drag
Reiulf Wilhemsen

Ruth & Reiulf in their home in Drammen

Ruth in her "bundet" that she sewed herself. These are special clothes that were worn for festive occasions in her area of Norway

Ruth & Reiulf home on a mountain—side in Drammen overlooking the city

Reiulf with his son Pedder and his two grandchildren. Pedder is in charge of a nearby mountain chalet.

Terje & Margrete Drag and family
children
Tore Drag
Hakon Drag
Elsie Drag
Torje is Ruth's son

Roger Stenberg and his wife Lina and son Ken. Rogers father was Tordis' oldest son who was brought up by our grandparents

Tordis Even Sternburg, Dad's sister. They had twelve children

Erik Stenberg, Tordis oldest son

Standing L-R
Caroline, Jarle, Andreas
Sitone, Erik & Elisebeth
Wilhelmsen, Peder, baby, Kristine

Front
Kristine w/ Erik & Hakor (Kjeti)
in China) Cecil w/ Sofie
Children left of Elisabeth
and her family children right

Picture taken at Erics new home Jarel, Andreas, Sitme, Hawkin Christen
& Kjetil. Kristen and her family are living in?? They are highly educated
engineers with the same degrees, work on the same project—they hope to
come back to Norway in about 2 years to live permanently. The ladies are
Eric's children

View of Erik & Elisebeth's home
from the front overlooking the bay

View from the deck

Erik & Elisabeth's living room overlooking the fjord

This is the home of Ivar Berg. It is
next to Erik & Elisabeth's

Back row:
Thale Anette Sydtskow
Mads Sydtskow Andresen
Torry Nygaard
Emilie Sydtskow Andresen
Janicke Sydtskow
Magnus Sydtskow Skjulestad
Tom Skjulestad
Simen Sydtskow Skjulestad
Runar Emgaard

Front Row:
Kaja Nygaard
Henrik Nygaard
Patrick Emgaard
Marcelina Emgaard

Ivar Berg—an early decendant of our family—has computorized ancestor which he use to help us. He was involved in the Norweigen air force

Eva & Erling Wilhelmsen Wedding at about 1947 in Drammen, Norway. Materials for the wedding dress were sent to Norway by Oscar Ellen and Andrew Adolphson. At that time, the war had ended shortly before.

Ivar seated in an antique Harvard War plane

Uncle Alfred Odegaarten w/ Blaine, Kathy, Dean,
Rhonda & Lorraine taken in 1964

Sitone and Jarl saying their vows at front of the church but cross way
to the congregation

Caroline & Andreas taken in 2010, Sitone's children

Elisebeth and two friends dressed in their costumes

Norm seated with Jarles father—He spoke good English

Norm standing beside bench celebrating the church's 300th anniverary in 1994

Norm, Elisebeth—Erik chatting

Stone and her sister Kristin who was bridesmaid

Wedding in Norway Sept 1, 1907

Norwegian Story

*The first communication we had from Norway after World War II was in 1946. They had come through the war quite well. Uncle Alfred lost his radio to the Gestapo German Military Police because they thought Erik(Lauritz) Sternberg was working in the Norwegian "underground" against the Nazis and he would not acknowledge it. Erik was indeed working for the "underground".

*Eva was planning to get married and she did not have a wedding dress, so Mom and Dad bought all the material and sent it to Norway. Eva later sent a wedding portrait of her and her husband, Erling. This was shortly after the war.

*In 1964 Uncle Alfred came to visit Dad and Uncle Andrew and the families. When he arrived in the Edmonton airport, there was nobody there to meet him. He had someone phone Dad. Uncle Andrew and I and Dad were supposed to be there but Dad misread the arrival time and we scrambled as quickly as we could to get there, which took about four hours.

*We picked up Uncle Alfred and Dad had a terrible time communicating in Norwegian. Uncle Andrew was much better at it. Dad would only say one or two Norwegian words and then switched to English, which would puzzle Uncle Alfred. In a matter of two or three days, Dad was doing much better with his Norwegian language.

*Uncle Alfred stayed for two or three weeks and we really enjoyed his visit. He had learned some English while in the U.S. but that had been over 50 years earlier. Some of it, however, was coming back to him. Near the end of his visit, he came to talk to me in English after he and the rest of the family had been over for a meal. Yutta had raised some "White Giant" chickens that summer, and he asked whether it was a roast chicken or turkey. One of his favorite saying was: "I'm fine and dandy."

*Uncle Alfred, Dad and Mom, Art and May Joy went on a trip to see the Bennett Dam in British Columbia, about 430 Kilometers away in the Rocky Mountains. He often commented on how the country was so big.

*He visited all the families in their homes and wanted to see what was going on at the farms. Dad brought him across the river on fjord with the tractor and visited us while we were fencing.

Pedersen Family

*Our grandmother Meta, who had returned to Dennark in 1932, came to visit her children: Ellen (Mom), George, Bill, Art and Ed in 1947. She had not seen them in fifteen years. She stayed for about six weeks and stayed with us for about two of those weeks on the farm. Dad was building the house that year and I was twelve years old. Dad wanted to work on the new house as much as possible so Art and I had to do as much farm work as we could. Grandmother thought we weren't old enough to do the things we were doing, such as bunching hay with two horses, hauling rocks and dirt with the tractor and shingling the roof. I could not see a problem with it, but she was concerned for our safety. She visited with Mom around the community and even attended a baptismal service conducted by Andrew Lundquist, at the Carl Swanson home.

*Before she left, I wanted to give her a going-away gift, and because of limited shopping opportunities in Valleyview, I bought a small pot with a short handle. When she opened the present, Mom said to me, "Watch out," and before I know it, Grandmother swept me up in her arms to hug and kiss me. I sure wasn't ready for that!

*She told us she had an operation on her bowels the year before her visit. She died of cancer the year after her visit.

Trip to Europe

*In the early 1960s, Mom, Janet, Uncle George and Aunt Amy, Uncle Bill and Aunt Viney, Uncle Ed and Aunt Esther went to Denmark to visit their home in Fredericia, which is an ancient, walled city.

*Their home was in terrible disrepair with nobody living in it. They stayed in a small hotel which was not very busy, and the clerk took an interest in them as they tried to find out if there were any relatives to be found. They did find one but he was not interested in seeing them. After a few days they left for home but Mom and Janet went on to Norway and visited there for a week.

They met with Ruth's husband, Tore, who died suddenly not long after. They also met Eva and her husband Erling, who was still healthy at the time. As well, they had opportunity to visit their son and his wife, Erik and Kari Wilhelmsen at that time.

*After they got home from their trip, there was a phone call from Mom's Uncle Sven in Denmark. By coincidence he had stopped at the same hotel in Fredericia where Mom, Janet and Mom's brothers stayed. The clerk started telling Uncle Sven about these people who had been visiting the city and their old home and looking for relatives. Sure enough, when the clerk told him the names, he replied that those were his brother's children. He excitedly made a phone call and made contact.

*He later came to visit Canada with his wife, Eva. The family had lost contact with him for many, many years. One of the things he asked about as they traveled here was who planted all those trees between Valleyview and Whitecourt.

*We drove him down to our swimming area on the river. The brome grass was just heading out and was higher than the car. He yelled for us to stop the car. He didn't want us running down all that good hay!

*Anneliese, her husband Erik, her mother Eva and their two daughters, Karen and Lana came to Canada to visit. Anneliese is Uncle Sven's daughter and is a school teacher.

They visited relatives in the Red Deer and Calgary areas as well as our families up north. Hulgar Madsen, from whom I was renting land, was also Danish so he enjoyed visiting with them as well.

*Erik Wilhemsen visited us in the 1980s on an arount-the-world business trip. He did not have much time but Art, Ken and I took him snowmobiling down by the river. Cavotec was a fairly new company, which he organized and in which he serves as president. The company sells equipment for deep-sea drilling as well as accessories, such as cable operator seats for large harbor cranes. He was then operating out of Drammen, Norway, moved to Charlotte, North Carolina, and he recently returned to Drammen to live in their new home and run his company

Our First Trip to Europe—Norm and Yutta

*I have been very interested in our family history and it is my hope that the rest of our family is interested as well, especially our children and grandchildren.

*In 1989 Yutta and I went to visit relatives and friends in Norway, Denmark and Germany. We landed in Holland and had a Euro Rail pass for a month, we used the train a lot. When we arrived at the airport in Amsterdam, I asked an employee how to get to the Amsterdam Central Railway Station, and she told us to "Take the Train." I looked around—I couldn't see one! So I suggested that perhaps she misunderstood me. She directed me to the escalator that we could go down to take the train from there. I learned from that experience that when trains go to airports or major cities, they go underground. They can do so because they are all electric—not diesel electric—so there is no pollution. All train stations are in the center of the cities.

*Once we got on the train bound for Norway, we were crossing northern Germany to Denmark. At the Danish border the German crew was replaced by a Danish crew. I went to sleep and when I awoke, we were on a ferry. They had quickly backed up the rear of the train onto the ferry, decoupled it and were backing the front half in, which only takes a few minutes. After we left Copenhagen, the same procedure was used when we entered Malmo, Sweden. When we arrived in Drammen we again met Erik Sitone, Kristen and Elisabeth, Reif and Ruth, and Eva and Erling. Erling was not very well by then and Eva cared for him.

*We stayed with Erik in his new house on the Drammen River. Erik was single at that time and was dating Elisabeth. Her two daughters, whom we also met, were similar ages to Erik's daughters and they got along very well, We were treated well and really enjoyed the visit.

*We went to Sande to see the birthplace of our Father and Uncle Andrew. The first place we stopped at was Uncle Alfred's cabin that he built, which I mentioned earlier. This was the last place our grandfather lived, and he died there as well. Unfortunately, it was locked and we could not get inside.

*We then saw the last house they lived in, which is on the seashore just above tide level. It was very handy for fishing. After our grandmother died of diabetes, grandfather moved to Alfred's cabin

*We then went to the General Store in Sande, which is still operating. This is the store at which Ole Boggan was killed by his car pinning him against the store.

*The school that Dad attended was close by. Because it was not in use, it was in disrepair. We have pictures from this part of our trip.

*We also saw the Holmenkollen ski jump; we even went up near the top. Boy was it a long way down! We were on the King's Palace grounds and also went to a very large park that had sculptures of naked people entwined into large tall towers. It is here that the much-photographed Angry Little Boy is displayed.

*We then went to visit the Sonja Henie Museum. She won the World's Figure Skating Championship some 40 to 50 years earlier. We also saw the large display of Thor Heyerdahl and his boat Kon-Tiki. He and his crew demonstrated how people from the Philippines and others could have spread their civilization throughout that region of the world.

*Norway is very beautiful with a jagged coastline with fjords (inland bodies of water connected to the North Sea), on which there are cabins and residences. They have a lot of tourists in the summer.

*We went to visit Agnes and Oskar Lunder, who lived about 50 miles north of Oslo. Art and I attended school with Agnes, and she later married Oskar. He had immigrated to Canada and was working in the oil patch. Art bought 650 c.c. BSA motorbike from him when he lived in Valleyview.

They moved back to Norway and acquired about 150 hectares of fairly new land that they continued to develop, doing things like installing weeping tiles to help drain the land. We spent two days there. One day while we were having coffee, a moose came running across the field. As it turned out, they they called it an elk. After we left Norway, we went to Denmark, our mother;s home country

*Hennig Christiansen, Holgar Madsen's nephew, met us at the railway station in Copenhagen. It was just a city block to Tivoli, which is a famous family entertainment park, which we enjoyed. We then went home to stay with Henning and Anna and their two children. Anna had a day care center in her home. They lived right next to a Lutheran minister. I will mention more about him later.

*We then went to visit Fredericia, Mom's home city in northern Denmark. Henning and Anna, Inger (Hennig's sister) and her husband Nils, took their tent trailers and we found a sign that read "Tenting." After we finally got there and got out of the car, we heard hymns being sung in English in a large tent. I told Hennig that I needed to go over there. He followed and when we got there, they switched to singing in Danish. When we came into the back of the huge tent, there was literature laid out on a table, some of which was in English. It turned out to be a group of Evangelical Lutherans who were trying to revive the State Lutheran Church. It was so uplifting just to hear those familiar hymns. How we missed hearing the Word!

*We were returning from a trip we made to northern Denmark to a point of land, Skaagen, where the Atlantic Ocean and the Baltic Sea met and mixed, which is quite visible. The area was a seaside resort. German bunkers were still in place—they were too well-built to dismantle. We visited a large country fair, with animals and large farm machinery displays at Aalborg, which was very interesting. We also saw a lot of pine trees that had been hand-planted on sand hills. These were being harvested for "pulp" wood. There were no natural forests in Denmark, only brush. They planted so many trees that they have enough wood for two pulp mills.

*We continued south on our way to Fredericia and visited the original Lego factory. They have many acres of land where they made villages of small Lego toy pieces that represented many countries of Europe. They captured the unique style of each country. They had an airport with several airplanes moving around. They had a small train to transport people throughout the area. Also included was a mock-up of Mount Rushmore with the four U. S.

Presidents on the mountainside. It is set up much like Disneyland in California.

*When we got to Fredericia we managed to find one relative who was a cousin of Mom's. She served us coffee and showed us her picture album.

*We visited the ancient wall and moat that had been built to defend the city. The history on this has been lost. We saw the very city gate that we had heard about in a story about George when he was 12 years old. The story has it that he was sitting above the gate and smoking a pipe when our grandmother came by and caught him in the act. But she did not confront him in public. We said our good-byes to Holgar Madsen's family.

*Then we went to Copenhagen suburb and visited Anneliese's mother, and her husband Erik, their two daughters, Karen and Lana and Anneliese's mother, Eva, Anneliese's father. Uncle Svend, who had died, was our grandfather's brother (who is mentioned earlier in the story). We stayed with them and they showed us the King's farm which was large with beautiful buildings and many, many deer. We also saw the Little Mermaid just offshore. It is quite small for a monument. We then went to an historical museum where old houses about 100 years old or more from all over Denmark were gathered into a village. There was a water-driven flour mill, a blacksmith shop, different styles of thatched roofs and various kinds of fences among other things. Anneliese's great-grandfather's home was also there.

*Erik worked for the Greenland Company and was one of the top officials. His office was located in Copenhagen where canals serve as streets just like in Venice, Italy. He would make a trip to Greenland, which is under Danish rule, at least once a year. They have a large fishery there.

*After this we boarded the train for Germany where Yutta's family comes from. I will write a bit about that separately.

Visits to and from Europe

*In August 1993. Sitone Wilhelmsen came to stay with us for about six months and then stayed with Mom for about four months. She went to Hillside High School and took English and Math. She was about 19 years old at the time. She mowed the lawn around the farmyard, which took about three hours, and enjoyed driving the snowmobile and the Honda quad. She also got a bit of and idea what grain farming was about. She would go to Debbie and Dean Adolphson's to be with horses, cleaning their hooves and currying them. The horses were in her control.

*Sitone rode a horse when she took part in an outdoor Christmas pageant, She represented Mary Mother of Jesus.

*I asked her if she had a boyfriend, but she indicated that she did not like boys and was not going to get married. So I figured it was fairly safe to tell her to invite me to her wedding and I would try to come. After 16 years she changed her mind, we got a wedding invitation, and I accepted.

*Alice Hennig, our sister, went to Norway for a visit and she met with Erik Wilhelmsen and attended his wedding to Elisabeth Heber. She also visited many of the people and places that I had visited and were known at that time. Elisabeth is a very competent horsewoman and had gone to major horse fairs as a judge in many parts of Europe, Russia and the U.S. When we visited them in Charlotte, North Carolina, I enjoyed observing her so skillfully handling her horse. You could tell the horse loved her.

*Ruth and Reiulf cam to visit our families in 2002. We showed them the places where our parents and Uncle Andrew had lived and worked and some of their accomplishments. It was a pleasure to have them. Rieulf was working for a Swiss electrical manufacturing company as a computer expert and taught throughout northern Europe until his retirement. Ruth worked for the school board in Drammen until she retired. The also have a modern cabin by the sea. Ruth sold her old one and they have a beautiful home overlooking Drammen River and valley and city below.

Visit to Norway (September 2007)

*Yutta and I were invited to Sitone Wilhelmsen and Jarles Fotland's wedding on September 1, 2007. Sitone is Erik Wilhemsen's oldest daughter, who stayed in Valleyview to go to school for a year as mentioned earlier. Besides fulfilling a promise to Sitone, I thought this would be a great opportunity to investigate more of my ancestry while there. I had indicated to Sitone's father that I would like to see the last house my father and Uncle Andrew lived in and find some relatives. Erik assured me that he would arrange to show me around my ancestral area (which he certainly did). Because of costs and the fact that this would not be of great interest to Yutta, we decided that I would travel there alone this time.

The Wedding

*The wedding took place a few miles north of Drammen in a beautiful stone church that was approximately 320 years old. The stone walls were about five feet thick but the windows allowed in an impressive amount of daylight.

*The whole ceremony was beautiful. Sitone wore a lovely flowing white wedding dress. Her hair piece complemented the dress nicely. She looked elegant! There were three bridesmaids and groomsmen. What was different than what I am used to was that the parents of the bride and groom also took part in the ceremony. They all stood at the front of the church together with the bridal party on one side and the minister on the other side, crosswise to the congregation.

*At the banquet, which was so beautifully decorated, the couple had many relatives, friends and co-workers present. The wedding cake stands out in my mind as being so beautiful and different than any I had seen before.

*We found the house my grandfather had rebuilt after Dad left Norway but that Uncle Andrew lived in. It was built so they could rent out rooms to to tourists during tourist season. It was two stories and surrounded by approximately two acres of land that was overgrown with trees and shrubs and not well looked after. It was, however, presently occupied. The railway station was about half a kilometer across a small field, which had a road running through it to the train station. It was probably about eight or ten kilometers to Sande from there. The station was called Holm and is no longer there.

*There were times when they traveled to town by train and other times when they walked. Dad was escorted to this train station by his father when he left for the United States.

*The house was located on an upper height of land, but below it, located not very far away, were Uncle Alfred's Cabin, as well as Ruth and Reiulf's cabin and Erik (Lauritz) Sternberg's cabin. They were all grouped set back a bit but overlooking the fjord where the boating, fishing and swimming took place.

Aunt Tordis and Uncle Even lived directly across the fjord and raised their 12 children there, except for Erik, who lived with his grandparents and one son who drowned as is mentioned.

*Erick Wilhelmsen was visiting with his new neighbor Ivar Berg and his wife Ashjoeng, (a painter), shortly after he bought their new home across the fjord from where our grandparents lived. He told Ivar that his cousin was coming from Canada and was interested in finding out about his ancestors. He said he had a computer program on his family's history in the area and if our ancestors lived there we were likely related. It turned out we were related a few generations back.

*When I arrived, Ivar was quite willing to share his information with us. I received recent information regarding Ivar and his wife. She passed away this past summer (2010) as a result of cancer. He has an avid interest in antique war planes, in which he is pictured in a Harvard two seater.

*He recently found he had distant relatives in northern Alberta and hopes to come and visit them and us next summer.

*Following are some of the highlights from the information that Ivar Berg gave me through his computer program.

*Our ancestry goes back well over 500 years in the Sande-Drammen area. People moved in from islands in the south, up the valley, and they usually did not move far from where they were born. People began to emigrate about 150 years ago. It is estimated that we have about 23,000 descendants in that area. People settled in that area as far back as 500 AD, so the 23,000 could be much higher.

*Lutheran Churches were the repository of records of people's births and deaths. The church in Sande burned in 1500 AD and all records previous to that date were lost.

*King Olav reigned in the 1030 era and grew up in the Sande area, so it is likely he is one of our ancestors. His nickname was Holy Olie. He was instrumental in introducing Christianity to Norway.

*Erik, Ivar and I drove out to the farm our ancestors had owned in the early 1500s. It was 10 or 15 kilometers from Sande, The present owners had a good house, holiday trailer, barn, sheds and other buildings. The owner was raising cattle, mainly feeders.

*The day we were there, he was loading manure onto a large spreader with a front-wheel drive assist John Deere tractor and loader. He had his manure spreader hooked up to a 130 horse-power John Deere tractor with front end assist and front end loader; both tractors were relatively new.

*He spoke English so I asked him if he was able to pay for all the equipment from the farm. He laughed as he said "No." He had a large industrial backhoe that he earned his living with, but he "just loved farming."

*This farm had burned down in 1918 but there was one building that was still standing, and supposed to be quite old.

*Then we went to Helmar Shervik's farm, which had a large hay storage area in it. The bridge to the top of the inside underneath the roof was still in place. The horses would pull the hay-laden wagon on a driveway suspended below the roof and the hay would roll off to the floor at the bottom—a distance of about 10 meters. Helmar moved back to Norway in 1923 and bought the farm. He had gone to the U. S. at the same time our father did.

*When Uncle Andrew was a small boy, he and some other children were playing on this elevated runway, and he fell off and landed below on the hard floor—no hay had been hauled yet. He was in bed several months—they couldn't afford to take him to a doctor! It was speculated that he would not walk again. He did have problems with his back all his life.

*Ruth and Reiulf took me to the Sande church graveyard where our grandparents were buried. Their graves had been removed because the lease for the grave plot had to be renewed every 20 years and it had not. They showed me the spot where the graves had been and there were several other relatives buried there as well.

*We also visited the Sande railroad station, which is now used as a restaurant and museum. We had lunch there and looked at some interesting artifacts. The village has developed into a town, with several new apartments and businesses there. The electric hydro generating station was gone, as was the original pulp mill.

*On my first visit, I was not able to see the interior of Uncle Alfred's cabin, but this time we got to look it over very well. The upper level had been expanded and modernized. There was a large deck added as well. There was a unique stairway built to minimize the amount of space needed. At the ground level there is a storage area in which the hand tools, used by our grandfather and Uncle Alfred were stored. They were mostly carpenter tools.

*A note about our relatives in Norway: as I mentioned earlier, Erik has a new beautiful home overlooking the fjord located on a large lot with access to the waterfront. Erick and Elisabeth, along with their two daughters and their husbands own a new log chalet in the mountains near Lillehammer, where the Olympics were held. It is large enough to accommodate all three families at once for winter outings.

*Sitone and Jarl have a beautiful home in the country. Sitone is working in an executive assistant position and Jarl was in charge of building a state-of-the-art hospital in Oslo, which is a multi-year project. They have two children, Andreas—4 and Caroline 1 year plus.

*Erik's second daughter Kristin and her husband Kjelit Sjolic are naval architects and have been working for a Norwegian company on ships under construction for three years in Shanghai, China. They just recently came home.

*They have two small boys, Hakkon and Erik.

*Elisabeth has two daughters from a previous marriage. She worked as a secretary for different companies. Her last job in Norway, before her and Erik moved to North America, was a financial controller. Elisabeth is an international F. E. I. judge in show-jumping for horses in many places across the world.

*Elisabeth's oldest daughter Kristine and Peder have one daughter. She has a Bachelor Degree in Real Estate and is working for a large company.

*Peder has a Master of Finance Degree and is working for I.R.M. as a Sales/Product Manager for heavy construction and mining equipment.

*Elisabeth's youngest daughter Cecille is single and is educated as a

Certified Nurse. After she worked for a hospital in Oslo, she is now working for a health insurance company.

*Ruth Drag and Reilf Whilhelmsen are retired and are in good health. They co-habit in a lovely house built on the mountainside and has a beautiful view of the city of Drammen.

*Ruth's only son Terje is married to Margret; and they have three children—Tore, Hakkon, and Elsie. They live in Oslo.

*Reiulf's son Pedder was working at a mountain resort nearby and has a wife and children. He has a responsible position.

*Ruth is our only living cousin in Norway. She worked for the Drammen School District for many years and retired from that position.

*Reiulf is trained as a computer consultant and was employed by a very large Swiss Electrical Company and traveled across northern Europe teaching programs until he retired. He continues to keep abreast of new technology in that area.

Some Personal Information on Erik Wilhelmsen:

*He is educated as a Certified Electrician in both high and low voltage. Erik worked as a designer of hydro power generators for a small European Company, then worked for 10 years as sales manager selling power supply equipment. He then started the Norwegian branch of Cavotec, a small European company and was President of the branch for 10 years. He then moved to Charlotte, North Carolina, and took over the U.S. operation of Cavotec. He was promoted to regional manager of the Americas' and then moved back to Norway in 2009 and continued to work for Cavotec. It is now listed on the New Zealand Stock Exchange.

*Cavotec is a supplier of equipment to "off shore" oil drilling operations and large equipment for loading and unloading large ships docked in harbors.

Families of Adolf Teodor Andreassen Odegaarten and Mina Mikkelsen Odegaarten

Adolf Teodor Andreassen Odegaarten (b. 1865, d. 1942)

m. Mina Mikkelsen (b. June 20, 1865, d. Mar. 12, 1934)

1) Alfred Adolfsen Odegaarten (b. Feb. 19, 1890, d. March 25, 1971)

2) Tordis Odegaarten (b. Aug. 31, 1892, d. July 15, 1955)

3) Anna Odegaarten (b. 1893, d. 1896)

4) Oskar Odegaarten (Oscar Adolphson)(b. Nov. 15, 1894, d. June 7, 1965)

5. Anders Odegaarten (Andrew Adolphson)(b. June 8, 1908, d. Apr. 9, 1982

(1) Alfred Adolfsen Odegaarten

m. Anna Amundson (b. Jan. 13, 1889, d. Jan. 13, 1962. They had two children:

1. Eva (b. May 18, 1920, d. Apr. 2, 1995)

m. Erling Wilhelmsen (b. Mar, 31, 1915, d. June 18, 1991. They had one son.

a) Erik (b. Dec. 21, 1950)

m.Kari Tone Nilsen (b. July 2, 1951) (divorced). They had two daughters.

i) Sitone (b. July 7, 1974)

m. Jarle Fotland (b. Aug. 10, 1974). They have two children.

* a) Andreas Wilhelmsen-Fotland (b. Feb. 26, 2006)

* b) Caroline Wilhelmsen-Fotland (b. Apr. 17, 2009)

ii) Kristin (b. Aug. 12, 1978)

* Living together with Kjetil Sjolie Strand, (b. Jan. 17, 1978).

They have two children.

* a) Hakkon Sjolie Whilhelmsen, (b. May 7, 2006)

* b) Erik Sjolie Wilhelmsen, (b. Aug. 27, 2009

Erik Wilhelmsen m. Elisabeth Heber, (b. May 3, 1949). She has two daughters from a previous marriage.

*2. Ruth, (b Oct. 14, 1929)

* m. Tore Drag, (b. June 18, 1929, d. Oct. 1, 1975. They had one son:

*   a) Terge Drag, (b. May 26, 1959)

          m. Margrete, (b. Jan. 15, 1961). They had three children:

*   i)Tore, (b. July 24, 1990

          ii) Hakkon (b. Oct. 22, 1992)

*   iii) Elise, (b. Nov. 8, 1995)

          Ruth co-habits with Reiulf Wilhelmsen

*3. Lauritz Engaard, (b. Jan. 19, 1913, d.) He was Anna Amundsen's son and thus half-brother to Eva and Ruth and step-son to Alfred Odegaarten.

(2) Tordis (Odegaarten) Stenberg
m. Even Stenberg(b. 1896, d. 1959). They had 12 children and about 21 grandchildren and great-grandchildren (birth dates are unavailable).

*1.Erik***	7. Solveig
*2. Adolf ***	8. Vera
*3. Gunvor***	9. Kjell
*4. Ove***	10. Knut
*5. Mary***	11. Elsie
*6. Thor***	12. Unnamed boy who drowned

*Tordis and Even lived across the fjord from her parents' at Skjonheim, Vestfold. She and Even are buried there.

*It is believed that there are no descendants of Tordis and Even in the local area of Drammen. Many are dead, but I am told there could be some in other areas of Norway.

*Oscar Adolphson (Oskar Odegaarten) married Ellen (Pedersen) They had 4 children in Canada-Norman, Arthur, Alice and Janet, all with families.

Our Danish Ancestry

L-R
Arthur, Herman, William, Edward George Meta & Ellen
Approx. 1925

Meta & Herman Pedersen shortly after they were
married

Mr. & Mrs. Madsen mother & father of Meta

Nils & Julia Pedersen at Silver Anniversary, parents of Herman & Sven Pedersen

Eva & Sven Pedersen in front of Elle Adolphson's home—1975

Karen & Lona & parents Erik & Annalise Tjustrup
Annalise is the daughte of Sven & Eva Pedersen

From Left
Erik Tjustrup Rhonda Reimer, Eva Pederson Andrew Adolphson Dean Adolphson Esther Pedersen
Ed Pedersen Ellen Adolphson Blaine Hennig Alice Hennig, May Joy Adolphson Art Adolphson, Yutta
Adolphson, Norman Adolphson Annelisa Tjustrup

Sitting
Bonalyn Hennig, Toni Adolphson, Lona Tjustrup, Karen Tjustrup Sonia Adolphson Lorraine Adolphson
Kathryn Adolphson, Debbie Adolphson

Adolphson Families.

Ellen Adolphson—1910- 2001
Mom

Oscar Adolphson 1892-1965
Dad

Andrew Adolphson, suitcase in hand, moving to Red Willow Lodge,
Valleyview, AB

Arthur, Andrew Oscar Adolphson Alfred Odegarten—3 brothers.

Martin Andersen's grave, Luthern Church Cemetary, Campia Wise. He was the brother of Adolf Odegarten. Oscar Adolphson stayed with him when he first immigrated to the U.S. He lent him money to buy a small farm in that area because he was a minor (under age). We visited Dad's farm that was owned by an Engnes a relative

The grave of an Engnes in Campia, Wisconson. He was a great uncle of Oscar Adolphson Norman, Bjorn Engnes, a Randy grandson of Adolph Engnes and Lorraine Adolphson

Edward Pedersen-   Ellen Adolphson   -William Pedersen
George Pedersen-   -Arthur Pedersen

L-R--Rhonda Adolphson, Janet Adolphson, Lorraine Adolphson

*We do not know much about our mother, Ellen Pedersen's ancestry. This is information that was received from a transliteration of a manuscript that was done in Denmark by Annelise Tjustrup (daughter of Svend Pedersen).

*Neils Christjan Pedersen was born on Nov. 14, 1858, In Egeskov Mark, Vejtby Sogn. He was baptized Jan. 9, 1859, in church in Fredericia, Denmark. It is possible that the above address for his birth would probably be a subdivision or smaller hamlet connected to Fredericia. He was married to Julie Sofie Ernestine Busse (b. Oct. 10, 1865, d. Dec. 8, 1928) on Nov. 8, 1885, in Hanover Germany.

*Neils apprenticed under his father who was a master tailor and then went to London enroute to Berlin to learn the art of fabric cutting. While in Germany, he met and married Julie Sofie Ernestine Busse. While they were in Hanover, Herman was born. It was a long and difficult journey to Fredericia traveling with a new baby. Julie never saw her parents again but had a visit from her sister and her sister's two daughters for their silver wedding anniversary.

*Neils set up shop in Fredericia where they had the store on the main floor and the living quarters on the top floor. He had a very successful business; employing six to seven workers and selling not only tailor-made clothing but also accessories for men and women.

*His youngest son, Svend, remembers: On June 19, 1919, at 9:00 in the morning, a very warm summer day, the home and business were burnt beyond repair. With the help of the neighbors and a few policemen, they were able to salvage bolts of fabric that had been imported from England and Germany plus other valuables and have a good sale. With the proceeds from the sale, Neils and Julie decided to buy a small villa in a cozy little village a short distance from Fredericia where they had many happy days.

*On Dec. 15, 1920, Neils had a stroke and died a few hours later. His body was transported back to Fredericia in a horse-drawn carriage. As they were laying his body in the ground, the sound of the pipe organ could be heard through open windows of the church. His obituary stated that Neils was remembered as a small, modest man who worked tirelessly for his church. He knew a walk of faith and prayer and walked amongst his family and friends quietly.

*Julie was remembered as a beautiful, intelligent woman who loved her music and did beautiful needle work. She would often entertain by singing some of her favorite songs from her homeland of Germany. When her children left home she would write them beautiful letters using the Gothic form of writing. She was well received by her Danish family but would often have trouble with some of the expressions of the language. After Neils died, she became very lonely and wanted to be closer to her family so she moved back into an apartment in Fredericia where she died following surgery.

*Neils and Julie had four sons: Herman (b. Dec. 20, 1885), Aage (b. Aug. 3, 1892), Paul (b. Feb. 14, 1897) and Svend (b. Nov. 30, 1902).

Herman Christjan Heinrich Conrad Peter Pedersen (b. Dec. 20, 1885, d.)

*Herman Pedersen was born in Hanover, Germany. He married Meta Katherine Madsen in Reykjvik, Iceland on Nov. 26, 1909. He apprenticed under his father to become a tailor. I will discuss his family a little later because he was my mother Ellen's father. He had three brothers.

Aage August Pedersen (b. Aug. 3, 1892, d. July 21, 1918)

*Aage Pedersen was born in Fredericia, Denmark. He married Zelma Christiansen and was a butcher in Copenhagen, Denmark. He died. July 21, 1918, in a military hospital.

Paul Ejner Pedersen (b. Feb. 14, 1897; (d. May 10, 1938)

*Paul Pedersen was also born in Fredericia, Denmark. He married Anna Marie Skov (b. Oct 6, 1896) on Aug. 14,1922. He was educated in Fredericia and worked in the general store where he sold clothing and dry goods. He served in the military in 1918. From 1922 to 1926 he owned and operated his own store. He died May 10, 1938.

Svend Julius Pedersen (b. Nov. 30, 1902)

*Svend married Eva Kirstine Andersen on May 19, 1940 and died about 1978. They had a daughter, Annelise. I talked about our visit to their home earlier.

*Svend was the youngest brother of our grandfather Herman. He is mentioned earlier in the story about when Ellen, Bill and Ed Pedersen went to Fredericia and was told about their visit.

Annelise Pedersen Tjustrup (b.)

*When we visited Annelise and Erik (b. Aug. 3, 1933) in 1989, Svend had already died but we did see Eva's home. Unfortunately Eva was away on holiday.

*As mentioned earlier, Erik's office was located where there were canals for streets and he worked for the Greenland Company, which is one of the oldest companies in the world marketing fish of all kinds supplied by the Inuit from Greenland.

*Annelise is trained as a school teacher. The whole family attended the family reunion at Don and Lois Pedersen's.

*They showed us interesting sites in Copenhagen, including the "Little Mermaid" and the King's Farm, which is quite large with wild deer and other animals running free.

*We toured the museum where they gathered homes of different regions of Denmark as well as a variety of shops; for example: a blacksmith shop, water-driven flour mill, different types of thatched roofs and different types of fences. Annelise's great-grandparent's home was also there, which was very special. The doors of that era were about five feet high. People's stature has increased about one foot in the last 125 years.

*With regard to language; the Copenhagen dialect is the national language. It is likewise in other countries because of radio and television communication.

*Annelise and Erik have two daughters: Karen and Lone. They both live near Copenhagen.

Karen Tjustrup (b. Sept. 9, 1966

*Karen married Manfred Muller in Austria in 2002 and divorced in 2007. They had known each other for 20 years. They have two daughters: Cornelia Muller-Tjustrup (b. June 21, 1999) and Carmen Muller-Tjustrup (b. Sept. 30, 2000). Karen lives in Farum (north of Copenhagen) with the girls. She has a job as key account manager in an organization in downtown Copenhagen.

Lone Tjustrup Olufsen (b. Jan. 11, 1967)

*Lone married Christian Skak Olufsen (b. Sept. 18, 1967). Christian has a son Frederik (now 19 years old) from his first marriage. Lone and Christian have two daughers: Martha Tjustrup Olufsen (b. Jan. 24, 1995) and Anna Tjustrup Olufsen (b. Jan. 15, 2000). Lone is a global communication manager in the medical firm Novo. Christian is a lawyer and they live in Holte (north Copenhagen)

*According to Annelise's story of Herman's ancestors, Uncle Svend studied in the London School of Dentistry.

Ellen (Pedersen) Adolphson

*Our mother's maternal grandmother was German, with dark, curly hair. According to Mom, she was fairly short-tempered. She came from northern Denmark where it bordered with Germany. This border was fought over through the years and it finally ended up in Denmark's possession, so her family lived in the era of border disputes. She died shortly after the last war at 88 years of age.

*Our great-grandfather on Grandfather's side would cut the hedges and dig around them and do some repair work. He was a retired tailor. I do not remember any mention of the other grandparents.

*Herman Pedersen ran away to Reykjavik, Iceland where he met a missionary by the name of Arthur Guk, who was a Brethren by persuasion. He married Meta Katherine Madsen in Iceland's first formal wedding on Nov. 6, 1909. Meta was the first to be baptized by immersion. Herman went to dentistry school. in Greenwich, London School of Dentistry. They moved back to Denmark shortly after that and he got into the tailor business and was very successful. Ellen and George were born in Denmark. They could afford a maid. They had five children: Ellen (1910-2002); George (1912-2009);

William (1914-2003); Arthur (1917-1995) and Edward (1919-1989)

*They moved back to Camrose around 1917 and started a tailor shop near the dam. William and Arthur were born here. Electric irons had just entered the market. Grandfather Herman bought one. One night he was awakened by a policeman telling him there was a glowing object in his office.

He and the policemen quickly went to the office to find the new iron had burnt its way through the ironing board and was suspended by the cord.

*After a few years in Camrose he moved to Davenport, Iowa to train for chiropractic. While in Davenport, Edward was born. Shortly after this time he moved to Maxia, Texas, to work in the oilfield. A well blew in and he got soaked in crude oil so he quit. We (Norm) drove on the outskirts of the city.

*He then moved his family back to Denmark and set up a chiropractic clinic. This apparently did not turn out too well, so he picked up his family and moved back to Camrose to set up a chiropractic clinic. (I understand that they fled the country because of the war and ended up in Camrose again where Herman wasn't allowed to practice because chiropractic was not recognized as a form of health care. In the meantime he functioned as a homeopathic care giver and also did tailoring again). But first he went to southern Alberta to work on the new St. Mary's irrigation dam. He apparently talked himself into a bit of a "boss" job. But when he fell into the fresh concrete and had to be fished out, he was fired. The Depression started shortly after that and the family was having a tough time financially. Mom was teaching and would help out some. Grandmother Meta moved back to Denmark in 1932 for various reasons.

*Our grandfather was a good talker and was the life of the party, which made him a popular fellow.

*Needless to say, it was hard on the children, moving from school to school in three different countries and switching from English to Danish and back. In spite of all this, Mom never lost a grade and graduated from the Camrose Normal School around 1930. She taught for a short time, substituting in the Camrose area but could not get a permanent job. She had an opportunity to teach in Valleyview in a new log school, one and three-quarter miles Northwest of 50th Street and 50 Avenue. She taught there for different periods but for less than two years. It was during this time that she met our Dad. She then went to Kingman, which is close to Camrose and taught for over a year. She and Dad got married July 19, 1934. Our grandfather Herman was at the wedding in Edmonton. They pushed his Model A Ford to get started, and drove off, and they never saw him again. He went back to Denmark; and joined our grandmother. He died during the war in 1943. *They went to an English Baptist Church because he was determined to learn the language well. He lived and exciting life and I am sure it was chaotic and hard on the family and grandmother at times.

*Ellen was the eldest, and as mentioned earlier, had four children with her husband Oscar: Norman, Arthur, Alice and Janet.

George & Amy Pedersen

Pedersen Coat of Arms

Harry & Bonnie Suetter, Sherwood Park Ab.

George & Amy Pedersen, Harry & Bonie Seutter,
Jess & Ryan

Ryan & Alyson Seutter

Jess & Christy Seutter, Julia, Autum & Zoe @ Disney World

Blanch & George wedding picture

Their son Allen, Bett & Walter, Comox, B.C. (Pedersen)

George Pedersen

*George married Blanche Jeglum in Ponoka. They had a son, Allen

(b. Feb. 20, 1939). They divorced when Allen was about five years old and he continued to live with his mother. She later married Walter Burrows, and Allen had a good relationship with his adopted father. They lived in the Camrose area as Allen grew up.

*After George divorced Blanche, he married Amy Erickson. They have one daughter, Bonnie (b. Apr. 30, 1949).

*George was a tailor by trade. This trade was handed down from his great-grandfather. He had two tailor shops—one in Ponoka and the other about two city blocks from the High Level Bridge and 109 Street in Edmonton, Alberta. He later built a nine-hole golf course at Ellerslie, which he and Amy operated for many years. Amy was living in the house prior to her death on

June 6, 2010.

*George loved hunting geese and ducks. He was a good conversationalist and he and Amy got along very well.

Allen Pedersen) b. Feb. 20, 1939

*Allen Pedersen joined the Canadian Air Force and earned his "wings" to pilot an F-18 fighter jet. As he advanced in age and experience, he got to pilot huge transport planes as well as helicopters with twin rotors when he was involved with air-sea rescue on the B. C. coast.

*When Allen was stationed at Moose Jaw, Saskatchewan, he was instructing air force pilots for five or six years. He married Bette and they began their family. They have three children: Richard, Walter and Melissa, Both Richard and Melissa are married and have children. They are all living in Comox, B. C. except Melissa, who lives in Ladysmith, B. C.

*Allen retired from the air force and enjoyed spending several years selling real estate in the Comox-Campbell River areas. He has since retired. He also enjoyed his family and was very devoted to Bette and their children.

His father died at age 97, leading an active life except for the last two years.

He died on Oct. 23, 2009.

*We, along with several other families, took our trailers and watched an air show at the Cold Lake, Alberta, air base for two or three days and visited with their family. The air show that year

was the largest in Canada and had a wide range of aircraft participating. We have also visited them in Comox, B. C., a few times.

Bonnie Pedersen & Harry Suetter (b. Apr. 30, 1949)

*Bonnie Pedersen grew up in Edmonton, living near the south side of the High Level Bridge where George had his Snappy Trailer Shop. He sold the store and built the Ravine View Golf Course at Ellerslie on a piece of property that lent itself for that purpose. The family has lived there in a house, part of which served as a lounge area. Amy continues to live there since George's passing.

*After Bonnie finished her education, she married Harry Suetter and they had a dairy farm south of Sherwood Park on Highway 14. They sold that but kept one quarter of pasture land, which they developed into a golf course called "Country Side Golf Course" on Highway 14.

*Bonnie and Harry have two children: Ryan and Jess

*Ryan manages the golf pro shop. His wife, Alyson, is a computer programmer, dietician and beauty control director.

*Jess manages the golf course maintenance and construction. He is married to Christy who is a dental hygienist. They have three Children: Zoe Anna (b. 2004), Autumn Joy (b. 2007) and Julie Katelyn (b. 2009).

*George and Amy helped them in the development stages of the golf course, which has 27 holes. As a CPGA golf professional and one who enjoyed people, George loved to marshal the course and help golfers with their game. He did this for over 20 years.

*Amy also loved to work at the golf course in the kitchen or washing the golf carts and wherever else she was needed.

Bryan, Ann, Bruce, Donald, Lavina, William & Ruth

Lavina Pedersen's 90th birthday, Bruce, Donald, Bryan, Ann Aunt Viney, Ruth

Viney & Alice

Aunt Viney & Uncle Bill Pedersen in front of their "Ginger Bread" house, Lacombe, Ab. (55 yrs)

Bill & Viney Pedersen

Family of William Pedersen - his Funeral

Ruth & Gordon Lennon Chritmas

Ruth & Gordon

Barbra & Gerry Nation

Harry & Brenda Mackelburger

Christopher & Danielle Lennon

Janet   Douglas   James & Donald   Bonnie
Macinnes   Pederson   Pederson   Seutter

Bonnie Pedersen

Ellen Adolphson
Amy Pedersen Adolphson
Norman Adolphson
David Pedersen
Gordon Lennon
Barbra Lennon
Wayne Pedersen
Dr Wm Pedersen
Jean Pedersen
Harry Sauter
Brenda Lennon
Doug Bansasco
Mabel Pedsen
Bruce Pedsen

Eva Pedersen

Arthur Pedersen
Alice Adolphson
Svend Pedersen
James Pedersen

George Pedersen

Lorne Wadlund
Lois Pedersen

Ann Pedersen

Bryan Pedersen
Denise Pedersen

Yutte Adolphson
Ken Hennig

May Joy Adolphson
Deanna Adolphson
Arthur Adolphson
Dean Adolphson
Lorraine Adolphson

Edward Pedersen
Dr Lavina Pedersen

Ruth Peders

Jess Sauter

Ryan Sauter

Pedersen
Gregory Hytta
Michlel Pedersen
Donalva
Freddie
Christopher
Pedersen

Sonia Adolphson Pedersen

Wadland
Keith Adolphson Wadlund

Blaine Hennig

Toni Adolphson

Katherine Adolphson

William Pedersen (b. 1914, d. Mar. 12, 2003)

(as told by his daughter Ruth)

*William Pedersen met Lavina (Viney) Cutland at a Baptist Church in Camrose. Viney had come to Camrose from Sylvan Lake to finish her high school. Here they met and fell in love. They were married in Red Deer on

Aug. 15, 1937. They lived in Camrose for a short while where Bill ran a service station with his brother Art while Viney did housework. From there they moved to Calgary where Bill worked at a leather tanning plant and Viney framed pictures so that they could save up enough money to go to Chiropractic School in Davenport, Iowa. When they had enough for their first year's tuition, they sent it on ahead and hitch-hiked across Canada. When they arrived in Regina, they encountered a gentleman that wanted a car transported to Toronto, so they ended up with transportation that far. When they arrived in Davenport they found an old house with many bedrooms and they rented it. Viney took in boarders while Bill worked at a service station in the evenings while going to school. On January 28, 1941, Ruth arrived and then it was back to Canada where they ended up in Bentley, Alberta. Bill set up a practice and Viney went on to Rimbey where she had a practice for three years. Don was born on June 8, 1944, and that was when Viney decided that being a fulltime homemaker and mother was her calling. That same year, Viney bought the house in Lacombe where they lived until 1998. Bill soon opened an office in Lacombe and then in Sylvan Lake where they went twice a week for many years, caring for the people in that community as well.

* They bought an old cabin on Brownlow's landing, Gull Lake and nine years later, moved it across the lake to Brewer's Beach where the family spent many wonderful happy summers boating, water skiing, riding horseback along the beach, having family reunions, meals around the barbecue and lots of company. Viney also had a large garden at the cabin and white fence around the acreage that was there for the sole purpose of keeping the boys busy and out of mischief but it really didn't work; they could find it without the fence.

*William served as a school trustee for one term and really felt it was important to have a vocational school in the town so his mission was to see this take place and he was able to accomplish this. He had a hobby of taking old buildings and restoring them and did this to several of the old businesses in downtown Lacombe. Bill had a passion for life and when he cared for his patients, it was not only their bodies that he was committed to but also the whole person, which was truly the philosophy of chiropractic in his time. He also had a great love for God's Word and studied it diligently and was either teaching a Sunday School class or preaching at some little community that didn't have a church.

*During the summer, on a warm evening at the lake, Bill would set up a movie screen. With his power plant and projector, he would show Moody Science films and people would come with their blankets and chairs and he would share his faith. It was here that Gordon Lennon found them and started to become acquainted with the family. Bill always said that Gordon was a gift to him for his daughter because he was a faithful witness.

*There were many wonderful times that Bill and Viney had together with Art, George and Eddy and their wives on their many fishing and hunting trips. The boys were very close and loved to compete with each other as well as play together.

*The fondest memories of my father were of coming down the stairs at night and seeing him with his Bible in his lap studying the scriptures. One of Dad's favorite Bible verses was: "God is my refuge and my fortress. In Him I trust". (Ps. 91:2).

*After Bill and Viney retired, they started going to Yuma, Arizona, with their motor home and motorcycle that they transported in a small trailer behind the motor home. They spent 18 wonderful years in the sun enjoying their years of retirement and many new and old friends. The last year they were down there, Bill fell off his bike and broke his hip. This was the beginning of his deterioration and the end of their travels. It was good while it lasted!

*They moved into a lovely seniors' facility where Bill stayed until Viney couldn't look after him any longer. A short time later he died in the nursing home in Red Deer, Alberta.

*William Pedersen died on Mar. 12, 2003. He was not only my father but my best friend.

*The following are the children of Bill and Viney: Ruth Elaine (b. Jan. 28, 1941), Donald Edward (b. June 8, 1944, Bruce (b. Apr. 8, 1951, Bryan (b. Apr. 8, 1951) and Ann (b. Apr 13, 1949)

Ruth Elaine (Pedersen) Lennon (b. Jan. 28, 1941)

*I have memories of a very busy, happy life. Mother spent a lot of time taking me to music lessons and teaching me in the ways of a woman. Summers were spent at Gull Lake helping care for the younger ones and riding horseback along the beach with one of our labs in tow. During the summer of 1957, Gordon James Lennon (b.) noticed that I had grown up and became very interested in a relationship and soon I became "Teacher's Pet." We courted for two years with his visiting every weekend from Calgary where he was teaching school and staying at the cabin which was not heated or insulated. So Dad took pity on him and gave him an oil heater. That had to be love! We were married on July 11, 1959, in Bentley, Alberta, and made our home in Calgary where Gordon took over the management of his father's business—Renfrew Motors—and I settled into becoming a full time homemaker. After the sale of the car business, Gordon became a developer of custom homes, duplexes and land development. Music was and is an important part of our lives: singing in the church choir and the Calgary Chorale Society and performing Handel's Messiah every Christmas for several years. We have been in several other choirs and I have had the privilege of doing solo work for many different occasions. For the first 14 years of our marriage, I spent every summer at Gull Lake with the children and Gordon would fly up on the weekends in his Cessna tripacer and land on the neighbour's field. It was great fun waiting to hear the plane arrive in the distance and then run out with a towel to wave and let him know that we would be right over to pick him up.

*While Gordon loved to ski and climb mountains, I kept busy sewing, knitting, gardening, teaching a lady's home Bible study group, being a guide for Pioneer Girls, being on the parent Council for the girl's school, and occasionally auditing courses at the University of Calgary. I love to travel and see the world and have been blessed in that our children have allowed me to tag along on some of their holidays and Gordon doesn't mind some alone time at home. In 1972, we built our home about 13 miles west of Calgary, in Springbank, where we now reside.

*It has been over 50 years that we have been married and we are blessed to still be in good health and very much in love with each other. Our children have been a blessing and we are now a family of 25 with eight grandchildren and nine great-grandchildren.

*The following are Ruth and Gordon Lennon's children: Barbara Lynn (b. Oct. 9, 1960), Brenda Ruth (b. Oct. 23, 1961) and Christopher James (b. Aug. 16, 1967).

Barbara Lynn (Lennon) Nation (b. Oct. 9, 1960)

*Barbara was married at 18, a year after high school graduation and living on her own in Calgary working in a daycare, to Gerry Harold Nation (b. Apr. 24, 1955). They met at Brentview Baptist Church one Sunday evening before Barbara went off to Prairie Bible School for Grad 11. Gerry was then working for the Calgary Police, so with shift work, they didn't cross paths again for almost two years. At that point, Gerry had given in to his true calling of finish carpentry and was doing his apprenticeship at Southern Alberta Institute of Technology. They married on July 7, 1979, at Altador Baptist Church in Calgary, followed by a short honeymoon to the mountains.

*Andrew Gerald Nation, their first son, arrived on February 18, 1980, followed 20 months later by Matthew Gordon (b. Oct. 19, 1981). They are as different as night and day but as close as two brothers can be.

*May 4, 1983, saw the arrival of the first of four daughters, Laura Lavina. Then along came Emily Ruth (b. Dec.2, 1984), giving them their royal family of two boys and two girls. On Dec. 20, 1955, Grace Ann arrived on the scene filling the void that was felt by Barb and Gerry—their quiver wasn't quite full at four . . . or five. Brooklyn Laura was the icing on the cake, being born to Laura on May 13, 1999, parented by Barb and Gerry from the week of 9/11 and transformed from granddaughter to daughter (adopted) on Sept. 6, 2002.

*You had better check where it is that Barb and Gerry hang their hats as they have had many an adventure building in and out of town with a four-year chapter in Lowe Farm, Manitoba, on 22 acres. Not only did it give them many new experiences, they also came back to Alberta with Daniel Steffen from Germany as their son-in-law. Their location changes but the strong family bond and faith in the One True Living God is always a constant.

*The nations just seem to multiply starting with grandson number one. Hayden William Nation (Bedford) (b. Aug. 8, 2000) was Andrew's first son. Then came Carmen Troung (b. Nov. 16,

2005). Andrew and Cheryl Anne Fiddler (b. Dec. 18, 1980) are expecting Chloe Jane sometime in the summer of 2010, joining their two families as Cheryl brings with her a son, Evan Fiddler (b. July 31, 2005).

*Born to Laura was Sarah Laura (b. Nov. 9, 2005), Josiah Matthew

(b. Aug. 31, 2007) and Judah Andrew (b. Aug. 31, 2007). They are all in the process of being adopted by Shaun and Diane McEwan, who Laura placed them with in May of 2008. We are privileged to live in a day of open adoptions and are still very much Grandma and Grandpa.

*Emily married Daniel Steff on Oct. 8, 2005, in Calgary, Alberta. Daniel is a mechanic and Emily is a stay-at-home mother of Jasmin Kathrina (b. Aug. 18, 2006), their perfect little miracle baby born at 28 weeks, which was three months early, at just over two pounds. Then Josephine Rose was born just five weeks early (Feb. 2, 2008), and Isaac Daniel born full-term (Feb. 27, 2010). The happy little family resides in Didsbury, Alberta, as does the rest of the family at this point in time.

*How much could a mother say about her brood, their many strengths and weaknesses—it would be a novel filled with joys and tears. It isn't finished yet though! We walk in faith until our Saviour returns or we meet Him with those that have gone on ahead on the other shore.

*Matthew attended Capernwray Bible School on Thetis Island, British Columbia, in 2007 to 2008. He loves being on his Harley or quad or hunting . . . . but he still hasn't found that wife yet!

*Grace is tall and true to her name, very graceful; loving classical music, playing piano and reading classical literature. She is well on her way to being a lifeguard, being held back only by her age. She loves being home-schooled.

*Brooklyn is also home-schooled, which frees her to follow her diverse interests, which are bugs and books

Brenda Ruth (Lennon) Maekelburger (b. Oct. 23, 1961)

*Brenda, born in Calgary, Alberta, is the middle child in the Lennon family—the one who loved to figure skate, play flute, play piano and sing in her early years. Many summers were spent at her grandparents' (William and Lavina Pedersen) cabin at Gull Lake. Little did she know that her future husband would also spend his summers on the same beach. Brenda Met

Harry Gunther Maekelburger through her church youth group after his completion of power engineering technologist—Southern Alberta Institute of Technology and as he began his mechanical engineering degree at University of Calgary. She asked him to escort her to her grade 12 graduation and after dating for four years (one of which Brenda spent traveling the U. S. and Canada with a music group based out of Chicago and recording a record in Nashville). Harry and Brenda were married on October 22, 1983, in Calgary, Alberta. They waited eight years before having children and then they were blessed with Trevor and Stephanie, 21 months apart.

*Both Trevor and Stephanie were diagnosed with absence seizures in their childhood and because there was no history of this on either side of the family, they were then used in a study out of London to research this extremely rare occurrence. Both grew out of them before they hit their teen years.

Donald and Lois Pedersen.

Evert Debbie Weenik, Dillon, Jaydon & Erica

Brad & Kelly Pedersen, Megan & Bretton

Becky & Darwin Carruthers, Caleb & Luke

*Trevor Donald (b. Aug. 5, 1991) is a young man who looks people in the eye, cares deeply for others and is eager to be an encourager. He loves music (playing piano, bass guitar, and singing), math, science and sports (especially volleyball and basketball). Trevor is also considering an engineering degree like his dad. In his room you find over 300 Hot Wheel Cars—a hobby he's had since early childhood.

*After a fall off a ladder where Brenda suffered a broken back and other injuries, her recovery was slow but nothing short of miraculous. During this time, her young four-year old daughter was shaped into what she is today.

*Stephanie Ruth (b. May 15, 1993) is a very caring young woman with a sensitive spirit to those who are hurting. She, too, is very musical, loves to sing, play piano and guitar and looks forward to possibly studying music for a year after high school before continuing further studies. Stephanie enjoys skating and baseball, but track and field is her sport, with her specialty being the 100-yard dash.

*Our family has a strong faith in God and whether we are singing as a family, in a men's quartet, in a church or college choir, doing solo work or participating on a worship team, music seems to be a great way to express what's in our hearts.

*Harry, who has a passion for steam trains and cheering on his kids, and Branda, who has been so blessed to be a stay-at-home mom to capture all the special moments that involves, recently celebrated 26 years of marriage. They look forward to many more years together as they watch their children grow and mature.

Christopher James Lennon (b. Aug. 16, 1967)

*Christopher performed his undergraduate studies at Trinity Western University,—University of British Columbia and the University of Calgary, where he was awarded a Master of Arts in Political Economics. He worked as a carpenter in the Pacific Gulf Islands of the Vancouver coast, rode a vintage motorcycle across India during a gap year and completed his studies in England where he achieved a Master of Science in city design and real estate economics at the London School of Economics. He met and married Danielle Maria Vander Byl (b. Sept. 24, 1981), a municipal planner from Smith Falls, Ontario, who had moved to Lacombe to work at the county planning office. Their wedding was October 26, 2006, in Puerto Vallarta, Mexico. Danielle holds an environmental design degree from the University of Waterloo where she was active in 4-H, ski clubs and family farm activities. Chris and Danielle are currently developing a 48-lot subdivision at the northeast end of Gull lake, called Deere Park.

Donald Edward Pedersen (b. June 8, 1944)

*Donald Edward Pedersen was born at the Lacombe General Hospital, the second child of William and Lavina Pedersen. He attended grade school and junior high in Lacombe and graduated from grade 12 at Prairie Bible institute in Three Hills, Alberta. After graduating, he worked two years on house and bridge construction, and then left for Toronto, Ontario, to attend the Canadian Chiropractic College. During this time he married Lois Carol Keller, a childhood acquaintance and she joined Donald in Toronto until he completed his Doctor of Chiropractic degree, graduating in 1969. After graduation, Don and Lois returned to Alberta to take up residence and set up practice. He enjoyed practicing chiropractic for 41 years.

*Donald served the Alberta Chiropractic Profession at various times as executive member, investigator and president. He also served the Canadian Chiropractic College as governor and the Canadian Chiropractic Association as executive member.

*Donald has had great pleasure serving as an elder and Bible teacher in several different church settings over the years. He also organized and ran a Bible boot camp, which was an outreach for youth and young adults in Red Deer, Alberta, for five years.

*Don and Lois are very proud parents of three outstanding children and seven grandchildren. Their oldest is Deborah Dawn Weenink (b. Nov. 27,

1970), their second oldest is Bradley Donald (b. Oct. 2, 1972) and their youngest is Rebekah Lois Carruthers (b. Nov. 27, 1970).

*Donald is a hunting and fishing enthusiast and also enjoys gardening and reading. He and Lois presently live on an acreage in the county of Lacombe, where they have resided for 34 years.

*Their daughter, Deborah Dawn Pederson was the oldest child of Donald and Lois who lived in Lacombe, Alberta. She grew up in Lacombe area and eventually went to the Lacombe Christian School where she met her husband, Evert Grant Weeninki, in grade one, They never dated until after graduating from high school in 1989. They were married on July 24th, 1993 in Red Deer, Alberta. They resided in Red Deer where he worked on the family's dairy farm and Deborah worked for her Dad at his Chiropractic clinic. Evert, eventually decided he wanted to be an entrepreneur and went and joined forces with Deborah's brother Brad Pedersen to form a distribution company, Deborah continued working for her Dad until her first child was born. Dillon Arian Weenink was born on March 12th, 2001. She then, retired from work to become a full-time "domestic engineer". Two years later, on March 10th, 2003 Jayden Donald Weenink was born. This was a bitter-sweet time for them, because Grandpa (Great-Grandpa), Dr. William Pedersen, passed away on March 11th of that same year.

*At this time Deborah and Evert decided to move to the country and bought their dream acreage where they planned to raise their boys. Then lo! and behold! on July 14th, 2005, little Erica Dawn Weenink was born. Now their family is complete.

*Two years later, Evert and Deborah decided to move to Campbellville, Ontario to embark on a new adventure. The distribution business they had helped grow; with partner Brad Pedersen, now became a manufacturing company of both toys and sporting goods. It was, therefore, necessary to move the head office in Mississauga, Ontario.

*Evert and Deborah currently live on an acreage on top of the Niagara Escarpment just 45 minutes west of Toronto in Cambelville. They have developed a new life of friends, activities and a wonderful new church family. Their children attend a county school called "Brookville Public School" where Dillon is in grade 4; Jayden in grade 2 and Erika is in senior kindergarten. **Deborah still stays at home to care for her children and take care of the home. Evert travels all over North America looking after sales and his accounts.

*On November 1, 1978 in Red Deer Rebekah Lois Pedersen was born. She is the third child. She grew up in the countryside of Lacombe County. In her early years she took busing to the Lacombe Christian School and completed her high school in Red deer at Notre Dame High School. After school she worked in her brothers' business for a while.

*On a warm Sunday afternoon she met Darwin Caruthers whom she married. They were wed on March 18, 2000.

*Darwin worked as an operator at Nova Chemicals in Joffree and Rebekah worked for Parkland Class, helping handicapped individuals.

*After five years of marriage they had their first child, Caleb Caruthers. He was a joy and delight to all. He is a thinker and a fixer of things.

*After two years a baby boy was born—his name is Luke Carruthers.

Luke brings joy and laughter to everyone he meets.

*After living in Red Deer for 10 years, The Carruther family took an opportunity to move out into the beautiful countryside of Lacombe County. They are currently living close to Don and Lois Pedersen and re-establishing a homestead that once belonged to Grandma Emma Keller.

*Darwin continues to work at the Nova Chemicals Plant at Joffree as an operator and Rebekah is the keeper of the house, raising two wonderful troopers along with pets.

Bruce & Susan Pedersen family. Wedding of their son David Nov 30/10

Bruce William Pedersen (b. Apr. 8, 1951

*Bruce Pedersen graduated from Lacombe Composite High School in 1969. He then trained as a chiropractor and practiced with his father. He then set up a practice in Three Hills, Alberta and met his wife Susan Marie Johnson (b. Apr. 10, 1956). They were married November 20, 1976, and have five children. Bruce loves the outdoor life, fishing and hunting and camping over a large area of Alberta. They had an acreage in partnership with his father at Nakusp, B. C. that they used during the summer.

*The family then moved to Whitehorse, Yukon, and Bruce set up a chiropractic practice there. He now has a new house with offices in it. Susan had been a housewife when her children were younger but got a job near Whitehorse.

*She and Bruce divorced and she moved back to the Red Deer area.

*Bruce raised the children in Whitehorse and they got their education in the "South", and some would return for summer jobs.

*Bruce is continuing to enjoy the varied outdoor activities of the area.

He has a twin brother Bryan. Bruce is the fourth chiropractor in the family, not including his grandfather.

*The following are the children of Bruce and Susan Pedersen:

Jodi Lynn (b. June 7, 1980). Jonathan Bruce (b. Apr. 24, 1982),

Tami Sue (b. Dec. 29, 1983), Sherri Ruth (b. Dec. 12, 1985 and

David Bryan (b. Feb. 28, 1988).

Jodi Lynn (Pedersen) Poelzer (b. June 7, 1980)

*Jodi completed her education at Prairie High School in 1998. She married Kenton Michael Poelzer (b. Sept. 12, 1980) on July 15, 2000. Kenton also complete his education at Prairie High School and received a Bachelor of Commerce degree from the University of Alberta, in 2005. Jodi and Kenton have three children: Carson Michael (b. April 1, 2005) Logan Alexander (b.June 21, 2007) and Devin Levi (b. Feb. 3, 2010.

Jonathan Bruce Pedersen (b. April 24, 1982

*Jonathan completed his education at Holy Rosary High School in June 2000. He married Tamara Nadette Larkin (b. Nov. 28, 1982) on May 31, 2008.

Tami Sue Pedersen (b. Dec. 29, 1983)

*Tami Sue completed high school at Hunting Hills High School in 2002 and received a Bachelor of Commerce degree from the University of Calgary in 2006.

Sherri Ruth Pedersen (b. Dec. 12, 1985)

*Sherri completed her high school education at Vanier High School in 2004 and graduated from Marvel College in 2006.

Bryan & Denise Pedersen

David Bryan Pedersen (b. Feb. 28, 1988)

*David completed high school at Vanier High School in 2006. He married Emily Rose Mackinnon (b. July 11, 1989), on May 24, 2009. Emily also graduated from Vanier High School.

Bryan Pedersen (b. Apr. 8, 1951

*Bryan, born in Lacombe, Alberta, married Denise (b. June 27, 1951, in Leoville, Saskatchewan) on June 12, 1971, and resides in Gibsons, British Columbia, on the Sunshine Coast, a peninsula east of Vancouver Island.

*Bryan has been employed by Howe Sound Pulp and Paper Mill for 11 years and is looking forward to retirement soon.

*Having been blessed with three wonderful children, their spouses and two beautiful grandchildren, we enjoy family time as much as possible.

*Bryan's passion for technology and music fills our home with hours of enjoyment. Together we enjoy gardening, biking, walking, our church family, friends, reading and traveling.

*The following are Bryan and Denise's children: Daniel (b. Oct. 26, 1971), Doreen (b. May 27, 1978) and Michael (b. Nov. 26, 1977

Daniel Bruce Pedersen, Sara Alison (Fisher) Pedesen

Daniel Pedersen (b. Oct. 26, 1971

*Daniel was born in Calgary, Alberta and Sara (b. Jan. 4, 1966 in Kingston, Ontario) got married on June 22, 1996 and reside in Port Moody, British Columbia. Daniel is a brilliant financial counselor. Sara shines in her profession as gynecologist and obstetrician at the Royal Columbia Hospital in New Westminster.

*Daniel benefits from Sara's great culinary skills and Sara appreciates Daniel "cheffing it out" after a long day in the O. R.

*Both Daniel and Sara connect with similar interests such as reading, theater, opera, dirt biking, working out at the gym and camping. Most of their travels continue to take them around the world as they plan to travel for two years on their motorcycles in a few year's time.

*A visit with Daniel and Sara is sure to be very interesting as they share some of their adventures and show where their travels have taken them.

*I have an assurance of my eternal destination which is prepared for us; which is heaven. There are many passages in Scripture that confirm this. All we have to do is truly believe. We need to ask for God's forgiveness for our sins past, present and future with honesty. He will give us the strength and the desire to follow Him and a peace comes over you and you start to see many things from a new vantage point, and have a living hope for eternity and I have a pattern for living my life and honoring Christ for what He has done for me and all those who accept Him.

Noree & Michaela Oldana—Kiana Bliss, Ezra Kia

Michaela (Pedersen) and Doren Aldana

*Doren was born in Edmonton, Alberta, He Married Michaela (b. Jan, 5, 1974, in Calgary, Alberta). They reside in North Vancouver with their two children, Kiara and Ezra.

*Doren is a marketing consultant with a web-based business that provides coaching and "done for you marketing solutions" for the mortgage industry. He is blessed to have a four-day work week and a thirty-second commute to and from his home office.

*Since becoming a mother, Michaela's life has dramatically changed from the fast pace of a professional photographer artist to falling in love all over again with home life. She is passionate about dancing, painting and of course, photographing her beautiful children.

*As a family they enjoy a vibrant multi-cultural church, music festivals, beach time, camping, reading and travel.

Michael Donald Pedersen, Ruth, Helena (Tikkanen) Pedersen

Michael Pedersen (b. Nov. 26, 1977)

*Michael was born in Calgary, Alberta. He married Ruth Tikkanen

(b. Sept. 30, 1982, in Sechelt, British Columbia) on Sept. 18, 2010. They reside in Port Moody, British Columbia.

*Michael owns an irrigation business. Being connected with "youth Unlimited," much of his time is also spent working with the youth. His big heart is welcomed.

*We are exited to welcome Ruth into our family and love her already.

She has studied in an aviation program at Prairie Bible Institute. She is Finnish and speaks Finnie. French is her choice in learning to speak a third language and is eagerly doing so.

*Michael and Ruth dream of having a family. Ruth says, "Ten children." Their free spirits will no doubt bring many adventures and travels.

Lorne & Ann Wedlund 2008

Top—Laura Centre—Darren Right—Krista
Left—Angela

Laura & Darren Carlson,
Sarah, Nathan, Halle & Cole

Krista & Marshall Harrod, Jessica & Anessa

Darren & Myra Wedlund

Ann (Pedersen) Wedlund (b. Apr. 13, 1949)

*Ann was born Barbara Ann. She married Lorne Paul Wedlund (b. June 1, 1948); on Feb. 7, 1970. Lorne is the owner/operator of LA Quality Trucking Ltd. He hauls feed to dairy farmers. Lorne grew up on a farm at the northeast end of Gull Lake. Ann is a stay-at-home mom and grandma. She is also the secretary for LA Quality Trucking Ltd.

*The following are Ann and Lorne's children: Laura Ann (b. Nov. 22, 1970) Darren Scott (b. Oct. 9, 1972), Krista Leanne (b. Jan. 1, 1977) and Angela Ruth-Marie (b. Apr. 30, 1987.

Laura Wedlund Carlson (b. Nov. 22, 1970)

*Laura married Darren Kenneth Carlson (b. Oct. 6, 1970), on December 13, 1993. They have four children: Sara Ann-Marie (b. Sept. 19, 1996), Nathan Darren (b. Mar. 20, 1999), Halle Laura (b. June 17, 2003) and Cole Kenneth (b. Dec. 17, 2005). Laura is an administrator at Inland Concrete and Darren is a self-employed truck driver and mechanic

Darren Wedlund (b. Oct. 9, 1972

*Darren married Myra Kristy Opden Dries (b. July 3, 1980), on January

3, 2004. They have two children: Tyler Scott: (b. Sept. 18, 2005) and Kaylee Rae (b. Oct. 5, 2008). Darren is owner/operator of LA Quality Trucking Ltd. and hauls feed to dairy farmers. Myra is a stay-at-home mom and hairdresser.

Krista Leanne (Wedlund) Harrod (b. Jan. 1, 1977)

*Krista married Marshall William Harrod (b. Nov. 7, 1974, on August 15,

1997. They have two children: Jessica Leanne (b. Mar. 19, 2001) and Anessa Krista (b. Apr. 28, 2004). Krista is a stay-at-home mom and is working on her teacher's degree. Marshall is a journeyman-carpenter working for Shunda Construction.

Angela Wedlund (b. Apr. 30, 1987

*Angela works in media services at the Red Deer General Hospital.

David, Maurice, James, Mabel, Art & Maryanne Pederson family

Mark & Kendra visit parents James & Marilyn

Back Row
Timoth, James

Front Row
Marily, Mark, Daniel, Christy

Tim & Missy, Christie & Ayena, James & Marilyn

Tim & Todd Pedersen

Arthur & Maryanne Pedersen, Lacombe Ab.

David, Maryane, Art, Jonathan, Jean,
Wayne Pedersen (3 generation)

Riley Madison Jesse Jean Elianna and Isabella Dec 2009.JPG

Bill & Art Pedersen's Garage & Service station in Camrose Ab—early '30's

Mark and Karen holding Jon's baby, 2008.JPG

Melody Pedersen & Jessie

Arthur Pedersen (b. July 21, 1917; d. June 17, 1995)

*Arthur (Art) Pedersen was born in Camrose, Alberta, and left soon thereafter for Denmark with the family. At the age of five, the family returned to the Camrose area. They came in winter and he wore his Danish shorts and suspenders to school, not knowing any English. When he was in grade 6, his parents abandoned the family. He never heard from them and ended up quitting school in grade 6 to take care of his younger brother, Eddie. He went to the Lutheran College in Camrose to find a place to stay. They took the two children in for about three months and then said they were a college and not an orphanage so they found a job for him. The two went to a farm where Dad was given very hard labor. In exchange for 16 hours of work per day, he could stay in the barn and was given food to eat. He hated the farmer and had deep hurts regarding his parents—so deep that he would not talk to anyone about it. Art's father was a chiropractor and plublic speaker. Apparently, he helped start the school of chiropractic in Toronto. Dad wanted to go to Valleyview with Eddie to visit his sister Ellen once, so they hopped a train with no food or money, The train only went part way, so they ended up walking for days. Upon arrival, they were fed and then slept for two days. His growing years were so painful that he never talked about any of it to any of his children

*Our mother Mary-Ann Strome, was born in Castor, Alberta, and was the oldest of 14 children. Dad and Mom met at Berean Bible College, where they were under the best of instructors—Ernest Manning (former premier of Alberta and daily speaker on Back to the Bible Broadcast), William Aberhart (also former premier of Alberta) and Cyril Hutchinson (founder of Berean Bible College.)

*They started a kids' club in their backyard where they sang gospel songs, did crafts and games and told Bible stories to a large number of kids. Mom and Dad's faith was very important. Over the years, every Sunday, they would pile all seven of us children into the truck cab and go to church (morning and evening services as well as any other services and special services that might be held during the week). The net result is that each of us children has a strong faith today and a desire to constantly learn from the Bible.

*Dad and Mom were married on December 31, 1939, in Calgary, by Rev. Gordon Skitch. Dad had taken a leave of absence for two to three days from the air force to get married.

*After they were married and had a short stint in the air force, Dad and Mom went to Rolling Hills, Alberta, to work for Ken Cassidy. He drove a tanker truck. He fell asleep at the wheel once and hit a bridge abutment and the truck caught fire. Exercising his abundant creativity, he somehow put out the fire and got the truck to it's destination. He tried planting peanuts and watermelons and a host of other things to see what would happen. He had a bit of an entrepreneurial spirit.

*From Rolling Hills, they went to Calgary and lived with the Skitches. From Calgary they went to Didsbury, then to Blackfalds, then to a farm between Blackfalds and Lacombe on Highway 2A and then to Lacombe. In Didsbury (early 1940s) he ran a hardware/lumber yard and built his

own house with a preserved wood foundation (one of the first in the area—the house still has one of the best foundations in the town). In the mid-forties, brother Bill asked Dad to run a lumber yard in Blackfalds. They hauled a granary into town and tried to turn it into a house, but then moved to a pastor;s manse. He started the lumber yard and ran it for a few years. At times, Mom would go to the lumber yard and find Dad on the floor—the start of many heart problems. He started to build houses while in Blackfalds and had quite a knack for carpentry. Although he only had a grade 6 education or less. He self-studied everything he could lay his hands on. He studied all the books for carpentry and challenged the provincial exam and got his journeyman papers. He even built a boat and fiberglassed it. He moved the family to a quarter section in 1957 where he could try raising and growing everything you can imagine. There was an old abandoned house which Dad thought would make a great chicken coop, so he got 500 chicks and heaters but the stupid chickens ran to the walls and all froze to death. Sheep were plentiful on the farm and when they gave birth, it was not uncommon to be hand fed. Consequently, many of them ended up in the house where the game of marbles became a major event. Due to the sheep, some of the older kids belonged to 4-H. Dad was doing carpentry on his own and people loved his work. His creativity showed many times. As an example, 30-40' glulam beams in Juniper Lodge in Lacombe were put in place single handedly without the use of special equipment. In the early 1970s they moved into Lacombe where he lifted an old house up and put a full basement under it and renovated it and changed the front entry location. He had a yard sale in Lacombe with Ken Cook as auctioneer and sold things most people would never imagine could even be sold. He decided one day that he needed a better way to get from one lake to another that had a small swamp/stream between them. So, he went to Texas and asked for a propeller blade and built his own swamp boat, which nicely got him through the isthmus many times on his fishing endeavours. After the sale, they bought a mobile home in Lacombe. Dad downsized and got rid of tons of stuff and sold or got rid of nearly everything. It seemed like he knew his time was drawing to an end and did not want others to have to sort it all out. He even bought a car and put it in Mom's name. He never gave up skiing though, until his mid-70s.

*Dad died of a massive heart attack on Father's day, (June 17, 1995) at 12:30 a.m. in the North Battleford, Saskatchewan Hospital at age of 77. He had had cancer and heart issues for many years. The loves of his life were reading, fishing, hunting and skiing. He was on his way home from a fishing trip at Reindeer Lake, Saskatchewan, when he had his heart attack. He drove himself to the hospital in North Battleford where he died seven days later. His ashes were buried in Lacombe, Alberta. After Dad Passed away, Mom moved into Canyon View Seniors' Home in Red Deer, Alberta

*Art and MaryAnn had five children: Morris Gordon (b. Aug, 1942),

Mabel Sylvia (b. Feb. 5, 1944), James (b. May 22, 1945, David (b. Sept. 17, 1947) and Wayne (b. Sept. 7, 1952).

Morris Gordon Pedersen (b. Aug. 5, 1942

*Morris Gordon Pedersen was the eldest of five children, born to Arthur and MaryAnn Pedersen in Medicine Hat, Alberta (the family was living in Rolling Hills, Alberta, at the time.

*Gordon was a chosen name because of Rev. Gordon Skitch, who officiated at Mom and Dad's wedding, and with whom they lived for a while after. I grew up in Didsbury and took Grades 1-8 in Blackfalds, Alberta. I went to high school in Lacombe, Alberta, taking Grades 9 and 10.

*Between the ages of eight and ten, we rode our bicycles to Red Deer every day for a week for Daily Vacation Bible School at the North Red Deer Alliance Church. James rode on the crossbar of my bicycle as we pedaled seven miles each day.

*When I was 12, we moved from Blackfalds to a farm 31/2 miles north of Blackfalds. I had to learn really fast about farming since I was a town slicker.

*As a young teen, Dad helped us to get five sheep each and we became members of the first 4-H sheep club in Lacombe. Our neighbor, Alf Stewart, showed us the ropes and it was a good experience for all of us.

*At the age of 16, we boys were playing with a sling rope, which was tied to a pulley at the peak of the barn. We would go to the hay loft and shinny up the rope until we got to the peak and then slide down the rope until we reached the ground. One day Dad warned us that the rope was fraying and that we could have an accident when it broke. But I went to the hay loft, grabbed the rope and shinnied all the way to the peak of the barn, which was about 32 feet!!! Then the rope broke. The impact almost knocked me out, and with my brothers standing near, they were in shock. So I yelled: "Don't just stand there! Get Mom!" The impact was so bad that all the muscles around my stomach and abdomen were stretched out like jelly. With months of therapy and not being able to sit or stand, I missed a lot of school. I was on crutches for a long time, so grade 10 was a write-off. I did not enjoy school at all so I entered the work force at a young age. I worked at various places of employment in Red Deer, Alberta.

*I married Carroll Wedlund on June 8, 1963, in Red Deer. We lived in Edmonton from 1963 to 1968, in Victoria, British Columbia from 1968 to 1971, and then returned to Red Deer in 1971. I moved to Regina, Saskatchewan, in 1972. We had one son, Robbin Dean (b. Oct. 6, 1964), who was born in Edmonton, Alberta. Robbin lives in Lacombe, Alberta with his wife Kathy and twin children, Kordan and Katelyn. His last name is Farrow. We had one daughter, Lavonne Grace (b. Nov. 19, 1969), who was born in Victoria, B. C. Lavonne married Gordon Sylvester on May 22, 1993, in Creston, B. C. They have two daughters: Amanda Lynn (b. Nov. 19, 1994 in Cranbrook, B. C) and Bethany Ann (b. May 16, 1998, in Kelowna, B.C.). Gordon owns his own business in Red Deer Called Fun Times Hobby & Cycle Shop. He has been in this business since he was in Cranbrook, B. C.

*I married Mary Rempel on June 8, 1974, in Regina, Saskatchewan, and we had one daughter, Janelle Dawn (b. Aug. 25, 1976, in Regina). Janelle and her husband Cory have two daughters: Adria and Alliah.

*I was employed by the federal government, public works Canada on October 21, 1983. I started as a maintenance operator in the Regina Post

Office and moved up the ladder very quickly and became a property manager for southern Saskatchewan. I was transferred to Winnipeg as a property manager in 1993, managing 51 buildings for Canada Post in Manitoba. I managed 500 buildings on behalf of Canada Post in Saskatchewan. I retired in August 1997 and moved back to Alberta.

*In 1999, I moved back to Red Deer, after being away for 27 years. I worked as a property manager in central Alberta with the provincial government for two years and managed 51 buildings.

*On May 21, 2001, I married Hazel Hill (b. Dec. 16, 1941) in Red Deer at Oriole Park Missionary Church

*I was hired by Laebon Homes as a warranty technician and gradually worked as a home building inspector and trouble shooter. With my multi-trade background, this became a good fit for me. I retired from Laebon Homes on

Apr. 7, 2009. We spent January and February 2008 in Yuma, Arizona. We went back there on October 3, 2009 and returned April 9, 2010. While we were away, we had a new home built in Blackfalds, Alberta

*Over the past few years, Hazel and I have had the privilege to cruise in the Eastern Caribbean, Alaska, Hawaii, and the Hawaiian Islands.

*Hazel has suffered from colon cancer and had two surgeries. Later, it went to her liver. She had major surgery at the Royal Alex Hospital in Edmonton to remove a large lobe, which left only a quarter of her liver. The Lord has certainly touched her body, thanks to a lot of prayers. We have enjoyed a good life together and enjoy all our grandchildren as well.

Mabel Sylvia (Pedersen) Schmidt (b. Feb. 5, 1994

*I was the second eldest child of Arthur and MaryAnn Pedersen, born in Lethbridge, Alberta, on February 5, 1944. I was named after Dad and Mom's very good friend, Mabel Skitch. Gordon was named after her husband. Mr. Skitch who was a pastor in Calgary. He married Dad and Mom on December

23, 1939. They also lived with them for a short while. Dad was in the air force and during the war he was stationed in Rolling Hills, Alberta, and was later transferred to Calgary. After the war, they moved to Didsbury. I was four years old then and I remember Grandma Pedersen (from Denmark) came to visit us. One Sunday morning we were all dressed for church and I ran through the freshly plowed garden and lost a lovely little black shoe. It was never found and I got a really sore bottom from that episode. It wasn't long and we moved to Lacombe and lived in Uncle Bill's basement until Dad got his feet on the ground. He then ran the Central Lumber and Hardware Company in Blackfalds. There was a grocery store attached which was run by Jim Baulkin and a suite above the store in which Dick and Alma Johns lived. Dick was Dad's book-keeper and helped him out in the hardware store. We lived in a small granary and Mom fixed it up really nice. Not long after that Dad rented the United Church manse, a two-storey house with a coal shed built onto the back. While living there (I was 12 years old), I contracted a nasty case of hepatitis—yellow Jaundice. I missed two months of school. Dad always brought groceries in bulk, especially dried fruit. He bought them by the case and stored them in a little room upstairs. The boys really liked to raid the little room.

*We moved to the farm just 3 1/2 miles south of Lacombe on the old

Highway 2A in 1957. I was 13. We caught the bus out on the highway to go to school in Lacombe. We raised sheep at that time and Dad had just given James a tiny little lamb for his birthday, which he called Lulu. One morning she followed us to the highway when we went to school and we didn't have time to take her back home. So when we got on the bus and looked back, she was running up and down the road crying and looking for us. Then we saw Mom coming down the lane to rescue her. Lulu was a wonderful pet.

*There was an old log house on the property (Olafsons were the former owners) with huge maple trees on the east and north side as well as a barn and other outbuildings. Dad added onto the tiny house that was there and the boys helped him tear down the old log house and one calm evening, all the neighbors came over and we had the biggest bonfire you ever did see! The boys were in their glory but Dad was a little nervous because the little house was so close.

*Dad loved to go to the auction and he bought some farm animals so us older kids were the first members of the first 4-H sheep club in Lacombe, which was started by our neighbour Alf Stewart.

*Dad still bought groceries by the bulk. He would buy several pounds of margarine (Blue Bonnet with the little packet of food coloring inside the box) and several pounds of butter and mixed the two together to make it go further. He used to mix together a large pail of Rogers Golden Syrup and a large pail of peanut butter. He also mixed together honey and peanut butter. The boys sure liked that on their sandwiches for school. Mother used to bake 14 loaves of bread twice a week. With baking, laundry and the garden, I don't think she had time for much else. Although, she did have a big garden and did a lot of canning in the summer.

*When I was 16, I spent some time in the Lacombe Hospital with double pneumonia.

*I left the farm in the summer of 1962. I was engaged when I was 17, with the understanding from my parents that I would not get married until after I turned 18. On December 8, 1962, I married Bob Lytle. During our first year, we moved 14 times, including back and forth from Red Deer to Calgary a few times. We moved back to Red Deer in 1964 and worked at the Provincial Training school.

*On July 15, 1965, Gregory Robert was born, I stayed home to be a mom and then on November 28, 1968, our second son, Brian Arthur was born. When Brian was 10 months old, I lost a baby girl that I had carried for seven months. *We bought our first home in 1967 on Overdown Drive in Red Deer. We were in negotiations with Bob Remington from Calgary during the next year and then decided to sell our house and invest the money in the Big Scoop in Calgary. So the move was on again, back to Calgary.

*The boys were picked up by the school bus at our door at 8:15 a.m. and they rode seven miles to Langivin School, which was by the General Hospital in northeast Calgary. They did not like that school and neither did I. In short, the Big Scoop could not support two families so Bob had to get a job. Word was out and Jack Donald talked to Bob about running Hannigan's in Red Deer. He arranged to have our mobile home moved to Red Deer into Mustang Acres. That was the easiest move I ever made!

*In 1976 we rented the mobile home out and bought a half-duplex on Hewson Avenue. A year later we were on the move again, this time to Kelowna, B. C. After 16 years, we were divorced. In 1978 I moved back to Red Deer. I worked at the Dairy Queen and on November 24, 1979, I married Roy Schmidt. He had raised seven children and two were still living at home, so we still had a houseful with Roy Jr., Linda, Greg and Brian. In 1982 I went to work at Banister & Thorn Insurance Company. The company was sold in 1984 so I went to work for Brewster Insurance Company. There were some changes going on there as well and I ended up working for Mooney Insurance Company. I worked there for 10 years and then went on CPP disability and it changed over to regular CPP when I turned 65.

*When I married Roy, he was working at the Advocate. We always lived in Red Deer and for the first time I had real stability in my life. Greg and Brian both graduated from Lindsay Thurber High School. We are proud of all our kids and especially the grandchildren.

James Pedersen (b. May 22, 1945

*I was the middle of the five children born to Art and MaryAnn Pedersen, the first of the post-war kids in our family. That should have been a time of great hope and expected prosperity as the nations were rebuilding. But it was a hard time for our family economically. After I started school and learned arithmetic, for some reason I took to heart that Mom and Dad had nothing extra to live on.

I recall how Mom wore clothing that was threadbare just to make sure us kids got something to go to school in that was warm. But I still hated wearing the bib overalls she made for us and for which other kids at school teased us.

*I was also, impacted by the rejection of other students because we didn't go to one of the two churches where we lived in Blackfalds. It wasn't all bad; we had some great times when kids in the village got together to play tag with us in the dark fall evenings. David and an Italian kid ran square into each other at full speed. One of them ended up with a very black eye. So I lived for the weekends when we went to church in Red Deer. Church became for me the place of social acceptance, the place where I learned to love the Bible and the people of God. It also set up some of my greatest inner conflicts.

*Mom seemed to see sins and faults in me so keenly. And as much as I wanted to obey and get away from that ever-present strap, I was bound to feel its magisterial power nearly every day. And even after Morris and Mabel took it one day and cut it into lots of little pieces, I was still hounded by my conscience:

I wasn't and couldn't be the kind of person I know God wanted me to be. Times of Bible reading and prayer around the supper table were fond memories. But by my early teens I was in despair. One day my depression was so great that Dad followed me out into the yard and asked me what the trouble was. I wanted to end my life but could not think of an easy way to do it. And Dad was helpless to respond because I wasn't willing to tell him what any of my specific issues were.

*Shortly after my 11th birthday, we moved to a small farm north of Blackfalds. I got a lamb for my birthday, so that was our first lawn mower that I can remember (not that we ever had any lawn!) I loved being there. There were lots of places to explore, endless fencing to do, sheep to buy so we could feed the local coyotes and chores that eventually transformed me out of a spindly kid into one who could (reluctantly) hustle hay bales. And we had a couple acres of garden and a raspberry patch that Mom slaved over. David and I did lots of work and playing together. We were given air rifles that effectively ended any prospect of using the hen house again after we shot out all the windows. But they were no deterrent to the seeming Millions of gophers we had.

*Through the turmoil of my teen years, I made an important discovery: I couldn't make enough "decisions" to satisfy God and change my life. The only thing that really made any difference was to confess and repent of my sins and then surrender my life unreservedly to God. Jesus doesn't take a back seat to anyone but He does wait for us to surrender. A small break came at a youth conference when I was in grade 11. But the real turnaround was after I married my American sweetheart, Marilyn, whom I met at Canadian Bible College. (No she wasn't the cause!) We went back to college and then began pastoral service in 1973 in Gull Lake, Saskatchewan. Four churches later, I was facing a mid-life crisis and went to seminary in hope of getting a new handle on life.

In 1990 we started 17 years of ministry in the U. S., during which time my wife Marilyn became a Christian bookstore manager (she earned some of the company's highest awards for her successes). It was also in Nebraska that I fell and broke my neck (C2 vertebra and three others in my spine). We lived for 14 months with no income but with the incredible grace and blessings of God that kept us going.

*The "nuts" that have fallen from our family tree have fallen in widely dispersed areas. We left a trail in some of the places we have lived. Having served small Alliance churches from 1973 to 2007, we left behind our eldest son Tim and his wife Missy in Palm Springs, California. They are now living in her dad's home where she can give him home care. Tim is a security systems installer. They have no children.

Mark, Maryln & James

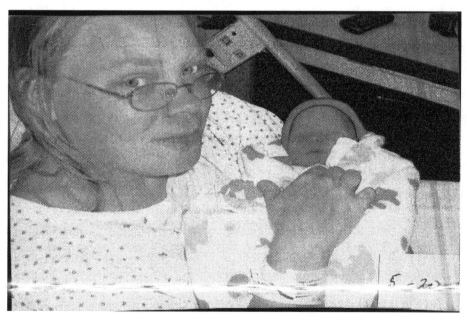

Tami—Dan wife w/new born Cabel Pedersen

*Our youngest son Mark and his wife Kendra, live in Culver City (greater Los Angeles), California. He has been trying to get his Bachelor's degree in Business Administration for about the past 11 years. His wife is an oncology x-ray technician and they too have no children.

*Our daughter is the second oldest of our tribe and lives with her four girls in Stony Plain, Alberta. Most of their family birthday's occur in December, so that adds to the confusion and fun at the Christmas season. An unfortunate part of this picture is that she and her husband are in marriage trouble so he (Todd) is currently living with us in Edmonton.

*Our middle son, Dan and his wife Tami, live in Hastings, NE, with their four month old son, Caleb. They struggle with the major economic downturn there, so getting by on part-time work, doing anything they can find.

*One of the greatest joys to us was moving to Edmonton in March 2007 and discovering after some time attending church there, that we were enjoying, not only the family of God, but our own relatives—Janet and Angus MacInnes! They have been a wonderful encouragement to us. And they are one more indication that God has been at work in the Pedersen clan, giving us an extended family and a desire to know and serve Him in this world. Individually there are sin problems but our hope and dependence are still in Christ. We pray for our kids when we see their struggles and praise God over all their successes.

David Pedersen (b. Sept. 17, 1947)

*I was born on September 17, 1947, in Didsbury, Alberta, the fourth child of Art and MaryAnn Pedersen. I don't recall any time in Didsbury. For me life started in Blackfalds. I received my first three grades of education there. A highlight of Blackfalds was when James and I would borrow a rather large homemade wagon and visit the village dump. We would haul back what we considered valuable items and Dad would have to load them up and haul them back.

*At age 10, we moved to the farm just north of Blackfalds and Dad wanted to try his hand at farming. One interesting thing that happened was the day Mother was angry at me and was going to give me a spanking, We started running around the dinning room table. Finally, I managed to get far enough ahead of her so I was on one side of the table and Mother was on the other. Then Mother let a little smirk be seen and I knew then I was off the hook, because a person doesn't spank someone when you are about to laugh. So mother said to me, "Sit on a chair." which I did gladly.

*The farm proved to be a valuable experience. Hockey on the slough, toboganning and skiing were pleasant memories. Putting up hay and making new fences in the summer, not to mention trying to weed an oversized garden and picking a commercial raspberry patch.

*After the farm, I worked at various jobs in lumber, oil and groceries. In the fall of 1969, I moved to Victoria, B. C., and worked at a discount grocery store. However, they paid discount wages, so I moved back to Lacombe in the spring of 1972. I tried other jobs, including real estate. One job

I worked at was a yard man at a farm machinery dealer in Red Deer. I unloaded new machinery and cleaned use equipment to get it ready for sale.

*And let us not forget a visit I made to Valleyview, Alberta. While there,

I was to be measured for a coffin. With tape measure in hand, May Joy Adolphson made it look very authentic. I was reclined back in the chair and

May Joy went through all the motions of measuring an arm, then a leg, Then she asked me to lift my leg high in the air. Before I knew it, water was coming down the inside of my pant leg, almost triggering water of a different sort! Everyone had a good laugh.

*When I was 28, I learned to play the trumpet. First I rented one because

I wasn't sure I could play it. The person who rented the instrument to me said I should see the bandmaster in Red Deer. Being very unsure of myself, I reluctantly saw him. He wrote out all the music scales I would need and after practicing every day, in six months I was playing songs. Now I use that talent to play in a band called Gospel Brass in Abbotsford, B. C.

*Jobs were scarce in Alberta in 1987 so I moved to Hamilton, Ontario, and stayed with my brother Wayne. I worked in various jobs of manufacturing overhead tube theaters, working with machinery parts and finally working in a hydraulic warehouse as shipper and receiver. The highlights of living in Hamilton were visiting Toronto Island Park, going to see the Toronto Blue Jays and the Maple Leafs' game and several times seeing the Welland Canal locks and Niagara Falls.

**In 1990, I moved back to Lacombe where I started my painting business. Actually, I feel the Lord started it. I was painting the exterior of my parents' home when a man walked down the street and asked if I did other painting. I said, "Well, I could, I guess." So he directed me to a commercial building in downtown Lacombe. My next paint job was an entire farmstead east of Lacombe. The business kept growing but sometimes I would have to work at other jobs when it was slow.

*In October 2003, I moved to Abbotsford and continued to paint, now in my twentieth year. I thoroughly enjoyed the weather and the people out here. As mentioned before, I play in a band of twenty people, called the Gospel Brass. We play in senior homes, in jails and for special occasions. Singing in the church choir and attending small groups occupies my time. When I first moved out here, I moved into a 55+ senior complex. I said to one person: "Everyone in here has a cane in their hand and I'm still on a skateboard." He told me, "Just stay on that skateboard and you'll soon have a cane in your hand too.

*Life is excellent here! This complex is divided into four buildings and each building, on rotation, puts on a breakfast, which is the first Wednesday of the month. Or we do one other function, which could be a barbecue or games night. This helps us to get to know one another and we become one big family. Life is great!

Wayne Arthur Pedersen

*I was born on September 7, 1952 at 9:00 a.m., weighing around eight pounds, the fifth and last child of Arthur and MayAnn Pedersen, in Lacombe, Alberta (affably spoken of as L.A.).

*The first five years of my life were spent in the big booming industrial hamlet of Blackfalds, Alberta. My brothers would take a large cream can and fetch water each week, carrying it between two of them at times; other times putting the can on a toboggan in the winter or on a moving cart when there was no snow but halfway between good walking and poor driving. Winter was the best time of year because it seemed like all the kids in town would bundle up and go tobogganing regularly on the hill behind Pastor Cornish's home. It had various degrees of slope and just enough bumps in the hill to add and element of danger. What would life be if you couldn't get hurt once in a while?

*Creativity flourished in our family and I helped it along as well. We were dining one evening (I was 3-4 years old) and I wanted another piece of bread. No point in bothering Mom for one as she had enough to do with the mob at the table and all the bedlam that ensued. Consequently, I went into the kitchen and tried to cut my own slice of bread (Mom always made homemade bread—not bragging, but of course the best). I had watched Mom many times so I knew the general technique. The slight drawback was the lack of personal instruction to enhance the observation skills. At that point, writing was not a forte so I had no idea if I was right or left-handed. I picked up the knife with my left hand and held the elusive loaf with my right hand, with my fingers liberally over the right end of the loaf. The result of trying to cut/hack/sever/chop the loaf of bread with fingers attached at the wrong end brought the discussion at the dining table to an abrupt halt much the same as a grenade going off in a military camp. The sight of my own blood mixed with bread did not help my disposition any either. Aren't scars supposed to enhance the human experience? No hospital trip—did they exist back then? A quick scolding, a good hug, liberal bandages and life moves forward.

*At the age of five, we moved to a farm between Blackfalds and Lacombe—so much to explore and so many animals from which to learn. What could be more exciting than feeding lambs with a bottle—wait—they can't wait—they start to suck on your pant legs and butt you as you laugh. There is a reason why turkeys are called stupid. I could hardly get out the door of the house without them chasing me and trying to peck me to death. Why don't they pick on their own size? Just because I was always tiny, it did not give them the right to peck (pick) on me. As if Dad's heart was not weak enough, one day I was in the barn nestled with a sow and her litter of eight tiny piglets. I never realized that Dad was a gymnast. He vaulted over the half-door and caught me up in his arms and sprinted for the door—rescuing me from a death that I doubted would ever happen. Didn't the sow love me? After all, I had never met an animal that I didn't love.

*Being so much younger than all my siblings meant I had lots of time to myself. Consequently, I developed a close relationship with nature and reveled in how God revealed himself in that manner. I learned how to track animals and figure out how they lived and how to predict weather. When I told Mom that I petted a deer one day out in the pasture, she smiled and said they were curious creatures. When I asked if I could bring a young deer home once, Dad said I could but it would probably jump the sheep pen fence and run away; which it did after two or three days. One day I told Mom that I could get within three feet of a beaver. She said that beavers were very timid and that it was unlikely. When I told her how to do it and got her within ten feet of one, she she did not doubt anything that happened with me in nature after that.

*It was always exciting to hear Dad tell stories of this hunting trips (big game or fowl). I longed for the day to go with him, but it never happened. One day, I took a pellet gun down to the slough behind the barn where the ducks came regularly—it was time to go hunting. My aim was good but a pellet gun is a bit weak for the distance required. Seventeen shots later, I proudly brought home what I thought would be a great supper. Major mistake—no license, not hunting season, too young, etc.

*During elementary school years, I went to camp a couple of times but was terribly homesick and didn't like it until the end of each week. Then, like many other kids, I wanted it to go on and not end. I loved vacation Bible School and any activity like it.

*By junior high, we had a huge raspberry patch. After working in it about two hours per day for three-four years, I learned to hate the raspberry patch. When coming home from school, there was nothing like the smell of freshly baked bread or cinnamon buns. Wow! Pavlov, eat your heart out. That would make a person salivate much faster than a bell. Then disaster struck—Mom went to work in Red Deer. No Mom at home when you came home from school—could there be anything worse that that feeling? It didn't seem right; she had always been there. Then, she developed breast cancer and the result of the radiation was that her right arm was permanently swollen to about three times its normal size. That arm looked like Popeye's arm. Dad also got cancer and ended up with the maximum radiation treatment. I went into high school wondering if I was going to lose one or both of my parents to cancer or heart problems.

*We went to church every Sunday as well as every special meeting that came along. I used to win Scripture memory contests at Sunday School regularly but the verses did not have any particular meaning to me. I was scared constantly because I thought Jesus would return at any time and I did not have a personal relationship with Him. I also thought I could not make that decision as everyone thought that I was a Christian and what would that look like? I felt as though I was in a "catch 22". I desperately wanted to have a relationship with Jesus as others in the family did, but thought it would be hypocritical to do so. When I was 12, Barry Moore came to Red Deer to hold evangelistic services. Of course, those still left on the farm had to go every day. Sunday, Monday, Tuesday—oh! relief, Wednesday had such a snowfall that we could not shovel the driveway out on time to make it. Thursday, Mom, Dave and I went. At the end of the evening, Barry preached on Hell and what the Bible taught about it and then extended the invitation time at the end of the service and pointed right at me (or so I thought) and said there were more that needed to come forward. I grabbed the chair in front of me so tightly that my knuckles turned white. Finally I could hang on no more. God was speaking to my heart and I knew I needed His forgiveness and the gift of eternal life that He was offering. I let go and started to go past Mom. To my surprise, instead of her being shocked and getting hysterical, she put her hand on my shoulder as I passed and said, "Way to go. I am proud of you." If I had known that would be the response, I would have made that decision long before. I was so relieved to get rid of the sin in my life and start on a journey for life with Jesus Christ. It is by far the best and most profound decision I have ever made. After that, I would take my Bible to school and read it and memorize it: only now the verses had meaning and I could relate to them.

*During high school, I went to youth group at church every Friday, youth prayer meeting on Tuesday and Christian Service Brigade (CSB) group designed for men and boys to learn life skills and provide role models for young men. At 17, I earned the highest award CSB had—the Herald of Christ. I also attended some of their advanced leadership training courses. I was the youngest in Canada to attend. Those years gave me the best concept of masculinity, manhood, fathering, life skills and Bible training that I could get. Later, after taking a diploma in Bible from Moody Bible Institute, I realized that the training form CSB did me well due to the depth of relationship that it provided. All through high school I was very shy. I would never talk to anyone at youth group on Fridays and only speak to someone at school if my name was attached to a question or unless they were a very close friend. This slowly got cured to some extent through courses in public speaking in university and Southern Alberta Institute of Technology.

*Higher education included a Bachelor of Science in Mathematics from the University of Alberta in Edmonton, Alberta, a diploma in Bible, a Bachelor of Education from the University of Calgary, a Master of Arts in Education from the University of Phoenix online and a multitude of leadership and evangelism courses as well as many courses and training in architecture from SAIT and the Royal Architectural Institute of Canada.

*While in the first year of college, I broke my leg skiing. Unfortunately, it would not heal. After seven months, the doctor quit and a specialist took over. He gave me three choices—amputation and prosthesis, leave the cast on and change it periodically for life, or do a bone graft with a fifty-fifty chance of working. I asked him if he knew Jesus Christ in a personal way. He said he did, so I told him to do the bone graft with 50 per cent from our end and 50 per cent from God's end. Today I thank God regularly for the gift of being able to walk, ski and do a host of other high energy activities. This was God's way of getting my attention. I was not allowed to do extracurricular activities in high school so went overboard in college. I ended up as president of Intervarsity Christian Fellowship, president of the chess club, running with the cross country team, playing on the bowling team, on the gymnastics team and too many other things as well. What a way to slow down-like stop. Friends tend to have sympathy for a short period of time and don't want gimps to hold them back, so over the course of a year, most of my friends went by the way. What a great way to have more time to spend in God's Word and build that relationship stronger.

*During that time, I went to a youth conference in Regina, Saskatchewan. One evening, the youth group decided to go a few blocks away to Dairy Queen. I started to go but realized I would not make it on time on crutches so I went back. In the cafeteria a shy young lady looked up at me and smiled. I instantly knew she was the one for me. Thirty-six years later, I still feel the same thing. What an awesome gal, Jean (b. Aug. 29, 1995) is. We had so much in common, starting with our shyness. Two years later (May 25, 1974) we got married in

Red Deer. It was my brother James first wedding to perform as a pastor. The first year of marriage, we had no car and lived in Calgary. We both went to

SAIT and walked to church (two to three blocks from where we lived).

*I was working in an architect's office full-time and doing a lot of volunteer work for CSB in Calgary. A couple years later, God called me into full-time missionary work with CSB. During the next 20 years, I trained men in leadership skills, spoke all over the country in various churches and Bible colleges and led a camp with all the responsibilities that that entails (camp board, government liaison, recruiting, summer program, promotions, etc.). While doing CSBI, I also did architectural work on the side and taught some high school courses on and off. After 20 years with CSBI, Olds Koinonia Christian School wanted me to teach there and do a curriculum overhaul. That lasted about seven years and then Red Deer wanted me on their staff. Thus, we moved to Red Deer and I taught Bible and math for five years until June 2009.

*In the change from CSB to teaching full-time, I got to fulfill one of my lifetime dreams—design, draw and build our own home. What a great experience! We moved into a twenty-foot holiday trailer for eight months and actually did the process twice before coming to Red Deer where we had a builder build most of our present home. In June 2009, we had three of our grandchildren move in with us and we have been taking care of them since that time due to some unfortunate circumstances beyond our control. What a wonderful way to restore the youthfulness in us! Who knows what the future holds?

*Our three children are: Jonathan (b. June 2, 1977), Melody (b. June 30, 1978) and Karen (b. Jan. 9, 1981),

Jonathan Pedersen (b. June 2, 1977)

*Jonathan is a journeyman steel and plate fitter. He married Stephanie Giebelhaus on May 5, 2003. They have three children: Madison (b. Apr. 23, 2007), Riley (b. Sept. 4, 2009) and a baby (due in the fall of 2010). They moved into a new house in Calgary in July 2010,

Melody Pedersen (b. June 30, 1978)

*Melody is in her second marriage and is currently in a very difficult situation. Her children are: Jesse (b. Mar. 23, 2001, identical twins Isabella and Etianna (b. Feb. 1, 2009) and Nadia (b. Jan. 14, 2010)

Karen (Pedersen) Stetson (b. Jan. 9, 1981)

*Karen is a a hairdresser and interior designer. She married Mark Stetson on May 5, 2001. They do not have any children and are in the process of building a house in Red Deer.

Edward Pedersen

*Edward (Ed) Pedersen came to live with Mom and Dad shortly after they got married in 1934. Ed was 14 at the time and he went to school on horseback sometimes. He finished Grade 8. The Depressions was on so it was hard to get a permanent job so he stayed with us until late fall 1942 when George found him a permanent job at a creamery in Ponoka, Alberta. Ed was promoted to manager in a few years' time and was transferred to other creameries. Later he started a dairy at Redwater, Alberta, and later sold that and worked with dairy-related business until he retired in Edmonton, Alberta. Around this time he divorced and married Esther Anderson, whom he first met at school in Valleyview. His first wife, also named Esther, was a nurse but did not practice too much after they married and had their son, Douglas. They eventually moved to Valleyview and I sold them three acres upon which to build a home. Ed died in 1989.

*When Ed stayed with us he was like an older brother to me. When Christmas came, there was always something under the tree for us kids.

Douglas Pedersen (b. Jan. 22, 1953)

*Douglas played hockey growing up and Ed was quite involved in supporting him. Douglas is now employed at Northern Alberta Institute of Technology (NAIT) as an electrical instructor. He and his wife, Patty, were married October 6, 1979. She has been employed at a staff recruitment agency until recently.

*They have two children: Lance (b. June 25, 1984) and Jennifer

(b. March 14, 1986).

depedersen@shaw.ca

*Lance is a high school teacher at Jasper Place High School in Edmonton.

Jennifer Pedersen (b. Mar. 14, 1986

*Jennifer is trained as a dental hygienist; and works at a private dental office for Capital Health in Edmonton as well.

*Thus ends the history of the Pedersen family.

Holger Madsen as a young man.

Above—Holger and Uncle Andrew visiting Torvald Gjile, Andrew's truck in the background

Henning, Anna, Jakob & Ida Christiansen

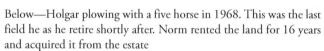
Below—Holgar plowing with a five horse in 1968. This was the last field he as he retire shortly after. Norm rented the land for 16 years and acquired it from the estate

Holger Madsen (Friend)

*Holger Madsen emigrated from Denmark to Canada in 1926. In 1928, he homesteaded a quarter section of land (half-mile square, containing 160 acres). Its legal description is SW12-70-22-W5. He built a log house, barn and other buildings as needed and secured a water supply.

*He worked on the farm clearing brush and trees by hand with an axe, saw and shovel. The larger trees had had their roots cut off so the breaking plow could pass through. Everyone did this until crawler tractors with blades appeared after 1945. After the land was cleared, it had to be broken (plowed) and disked and the roots picked so it was ready for crop the following year. He usually cleared and broke 5-10 acres per year. He had no horses or machinery so he exchanged work or cash with neighbours who had horses and machinery. He continued this until 1942 when he bought his own horses and machinery but hired the crops to be threshed and later combined.

*Up until 1941, he worked in the winter for Saskatchewan farmers with livestock. Jobs were hard to get and the pay was poor.

*His land was fertile and he got reasonable crops and he also had a small herd of cattle and some pigs and was quite successful.

*He farmed continuously with horses until he retired in about 1963. Then I rented the land for 21 years until he died.

*He had no family in Canada so he was like a family member to us. He really liked children and always had treats for them.

*Holger's sister, nephew, niece and her husband visited him in the early 1980s. We got to know them quite well and when Holger died, Henning and Anna, his nephew and niece Inger came here for the funeral and Hennig gave the eulogy.

*There is more of the story included in our trip to Denmark.

*In 1989, we visited Denmark, Norway and Germany. Henning and Anna met us at the train station in Copenhagen and we spent a week in Copenhagen, Fredericia and the northern parts of Denmark as well as Ingstrup area, which is near where Holger's home was and where his parents are buried. We also visited other relatives of his that lived nearby.

Holger's sister was the mother of Henning and Inger. Nils was Inger's husband. They spent a week showing us many parts of Denmark, which is described in our visit to Denmark.

Henning and Anna Christiansen's children: Jakob (b. July 17. 1978) and Ida (b. Oct. 7, 1982.

Jakob Christiansen (b. July 17, 1978

Jakob is trained as a fundraiser and works nearby. He also has a degree in Science (Humanities). He is living with Soren Feldtfos Thomsen, who has the same education as Jakob,

Ida Christiansen (b. Oct. 7, 1982)

Ida teaches school in Auning, a nearby town. She is living with Sune Schlizther and he teaches in the same school.

The Klumbies Family

The history that is known about this family is relatively short. The first and second world wars disrupted the families somewhat because they were living apart from Lithuania to southern Germany, close to Stuttgart.

Yutta's mother, Madeline Schneider, lost her mother when she was quite young. Madeline's father married another woman and she felt her stepmother did not treat her very well so she left home at a young age and worked on farms until she met Wilhelm (Bill) Klumbies.

Bill Klumbies worked for farmers and in a brick yard before he acquired a bus to transport people from place to place. When the war started it became more and more difficult to buy Gasoline for the bus.

To solve that problem he put a wood stove at the back of the bus and ran tubing to the engine in front to pipe the unburned methane gases for fuel. The passengers added wood to the fire as it was needed. He ran the bus until he was conscripted into the German army. He served as a valet for a lieutenant, preparing meals, driving a nice car, servicing the car and looking after his employer's clothing.

When the German army attacked the Russians, he and the army were drawn deep into Russia into a trap devised by the allies and they encircled the

German Heritage

Wilhelm & Madeline Klumbies

Kurt, Yutta, Madeline & Bill

Kurt, "Bill, Yutta

Klumbies family in ship dining room coming to Canada

Alvin, Sharon, Chloe, Libby, Sawyer, Hudson, Thomas children listed by age. Reside in St. Albert, Ab.

Friedel-Cousin Yutta, Uncle Max is Yutta's mother's brother. They live in Kettwig, Germany

Brenda, Helma, Kurt, Diane & Sharon

L—Rhonda, Lorraine, Sonie Adolphson

R—Diane, Brenda, Sharon Klumbies

Aunt Eva, Yutta, Madeline sisters

Lorraine, Rhonda, Diane, Brenda, Sonia, Sharon

German army in -30 to -40 degrees Celsius temperatures and deep snow.

Most of the army surrendered and were taken prisoner. Some died of hunger and exposure.

*Bill managed to get away on foot and get back to German territory. He did not seem to want to talk about it so he probably had to do things he didn't want to talk about, just to survive. He went cross-country for over a thousand miles (1600 kilometers) trying to feed himself while being hunted by the Russians. He liked to talk about the funny things that happened, such as the time when they moved camp and set up again and they placed the toilets at the back of the camp. Over one toilet, the sign read "Officers" and on the other sign it read, "For the other assholes."

*Another saying in the German army was about the Italian army with which they were allied—the Italian tanks had four reverses and one forward gear.

*During the war, Madeline had to provide for Kurt and Yutta. She managed to find work and send Kurt to school until near the end of the war.

*She got a real scare when two Russian soldiers came to the door and asked to enter the house. They were hungry and dirty and requested eggs and other food. One of them could speak a bit of German and said they were sorry for intruding but that the Russian army was a bit disorganized. They also put on Bill's woolen underwear.

*A little later as the Russians occupied the area, she was ordered to help dismantle factories and items of value that were put on rail cars and hauled to Russia. The last thing they loaded on the rail cars were the rails as the train moved forward slowly.

*Yutta would watch for her mother every evening because she was scared that her mother might not come home. She had heard of the Russians rounding up able-bodied people and hauling them to labour camps deep in Russia.

*They were now living in East Germany and Madeline wanted to get to West Germany. They were among the many refugees that wanted to cross the border to meet Bill. In order to get across, Madeline lay on the bottom of a truck box and they piled suit cases around her and whatever else they could find to conceal her. Yutta and Kurt were also with her in the back of the truck.

It was a short distance across the border; otherwise Madeline would have been asphyxiated.

*Bill was promised a job on a farm by his lieutenant when he returned to Germany. Both he and Madeline were looking for one another in the same city at the same time. A short time later the Red Cross arranged to get them together. They then went to the farm that Bill's army boss owned and he worked there for a while. He then got a job at a brick factory and worked there until he immigrated with his family to Canada.

*Bill lost a brother, Ernst, in the war. His wife stayed in East Germany and he had one son, Gunther, who is married and lives in Lithuania. Gunther contacted the family through his mother and Yutta wrote to him but he didn't respond. Bill also had a sister, Marie, and her husband, Valentine, and brother, Bruno who had no family of their own,

*Marie and Valentine (Valley) visited the family in Canada in the 1970s.

*Madeline Schneider had two brothers; Max and Hans, and a sister, Eva.

Max Schneider

*Max had three children: Friedel, Crystal and Wilma

*Friedel and his wife Ushi had no children but had one dog they named *Biggy. We stayed with them when we visited there in 1989.

*Crystal and her husband, Gunther had three sons.

*Wilma had one son and one daughter.

Hans Schneider

*Hans was a widower with one grown step-daughter. He was also Madeline Klumbies' brother.

Eva Schneider

*Eva continued to live in East Germany close to the grave of her six year old daughter, Edith. Madeline saw her after the war when she visited them in West Germany. She lost her husband in the war.

*All have died, except Crystal and her three sons, Wilma's children and Ushi. They all live in Kettwig close to Dusseldorf on the Rhine River.

*Friedel, together with Crystal's husband had a small factory where they electromagnetically painted black body parts for Volkswagen, Ope and other car manufacturers. The last I heard was that Crystal's son was running the factory.

Sharon Corinne Thomas (Klumbies) Born November 26. 1969 in Edmonton AB

Alvin Konrad Thomas Born May 24. 1964 in Mandeville, Jamaica

Chloe Ainsley Thomas born August 9. 1994

Libby Geneva thomas. born April 24. 1996

Sawyer Jett Thomas. Born April 30. 2002

Hudson Seth Thomas. Born March 10. 2005

Alvin and I were engaged July 10. 1992 and married April 24. 1993.

Alvin is presently in the Real Estate business and Sharon has been involved in the same business as an agent, to a lesser degree as the family grew.

GOING TO CANADA!

*Yutta's mother and father just could not get ahead financially and considered immigrating to Australia or Canada. They chose Canada, partly because it was closer to Germany. They got assistance from the North American Baptist Conference, who had a department that specialized in settling German immigrants. They were supposed to work in the sugar beet fields in southern Alberta but arrived after the season was over. They were then sent to Valleview where the Jake Lehman family took them into their home until they were able to rent their own house in the town of Valleyview.

*I need to go back a bit in time . . . . Rev. Stuhrhan represented the North American Baptist Conference in their effort to assist German immigrants to settle in Canada and he was in charge of the Klumbies family's immigration.

*They sailed on the Arosa Star, which was carrying immigrants of mostly German descent and landed in Quebec City. They took the train from there to Edmonton and then onto High Prairie.

*They had heard erroneously that there were certain items you could not buy in Canada, such as sewing machines and dishes, so they needlessly transported some of these items along with them.

*Yutta's mother worked as a cook in several restaurants over the years as well as at Sturgeon Lake Bible Camp.

*Yuttas's father worked for the power company for a short time and then worked for Flint Rig as a labourer and later as a foreman for a total of about 17 years.

*They arrived in Canada in 1954. In 1956 he bought a lot from Oscar Adolphson and started to build a house that they would finish over five or six years. They didn't have much debt and they didn't have a vehicle for about three years after coming to Canada. They thought Canada was a great place to live.

*They were good supporters of Emmanuel Baptist Church and were very serious about their Christian commitment.

*They visited relatives in Germany in 1972, but Canada had become their home by choice.

*Bill and Madeline retired and moved to Edmonton in 1973. They both had relatively good health to the end. Our girls all loved visiting them both in Valleyview and Edmonton. Oma was an excellent cook, loved to entertain and had surprises for us all.

*Bill died in 1982 and Madeline died in 1988. They are both buried in Sherwood Park, Alberta

*Yutta's grandfather's name was Adam and her grandmother's name was Marie. These were her father's parents. She didn't get to know them very well because they lived some distance away.

*Yutta Rita Klumbies, married Norman Henry Adolphson on Oct. 25, 1958, and have three daughters: Rhonda (b. June 16, 1959), Lorraine Ann (b. Dec.

26, 1961) and Sonia Fay (b. Dec, 8, 1966).

*Yutta was a homemaker and occasionally worked at a government office as a clerk. She worked on the farm, operating machinery in spring and fall when we did not have a hired man. She also drove the girls to piano lessons, school and church activities.

Kurt Klumbies (b. Sept. 1934)

*I saw, as a five-year old boy, the start of World War I. We had to move

15 kilometers back to Grandpa Schneider's farm. Since we were only one kilometer from the Lithuanian border and Russia was at the border, there we could see and hear the war start.

*My grandfather Klumbies' farm was partly burned down since the Russians burned as much as they could on their way back.

*When the war came slowly to an end, my dad made a secret deal by mail to move the family to Brandenburg, which was about 90 kilometers from Berlin and we could see the fireworks over Berlin. But on May 5, 1945, we ended up in the Russian sector of Germany.

*Dad ended up on the British side without being captured by the Russians. After everything had settled and the mail started to flow again, he contacted us from Detmold, West Germany, where he was on a farm owned by his "Feldwebel." He had been his driver for many years in the war.

*In 1946, Mom, Yutta and I had to get a visa from the Russians to get over the border. We could cross only by horse and wagon with two to three families per wagon. This was a special crossing

that was supervised by the Russians. But we made it across and once we were on the west side we took the train to Detmold.

*Here the family was together and Dad worked on the farm and we had two rooms in the big farmhouse! Here we started school again and had to walk 4 kilometers. The German Mark was worthless here and shortly after we had a correction, 100 old Mark became 1 new Mark and the economy started up again. In 1949, I was 15 1/2 years old, and I started as a plumber and sheet metal apprentice in the city, which was an 11-kilometer bus ride from the farm. At the end we had a bike to get around. The bus fare was more than what a first-year apprentice would earn a week. We went about four kilometers to the next streetcar station and then another four kilometers to the nearest Baptist church in Horn. Dad could also earn a lot more by moving to the industrial cities like Dusseldorf, and that was our next move in the 1950s. Here he worked at the brick factory and was delivering bricks with two trailers behind an old Mack army truck. To keep the brick ovens going, he also trucked in coal from the coal-producing cities like Essen.

*I continued my apprenticeship again and finished in mid-1952. The rebuilding of Dusseldorf after the war was a big task. I bought a motor bike and traveled a lot with a friend who had a scooter. But the motorbike gave me bad arthritis in my left shoulder . . . I was dressed properly and had to have a sudden unexpected stomach operation from the rough ride on it. The evening before I drank 11 cups of tea at my aunt's house. Then we traveled home with Yutta and in the morning I was in the hospital on the operating table. The operation delayed our immigration to Canada by one year. I recovered from it very well but had only one-third of my stomach left.

*In July 1954, we went to Bramen and in one week had to go through all legal preparations to leave on the Arosa Star to Quebec. We left late in the evening from Bremer Haven and during our first dinner we were on the North Sea to Britain. But a storm came up and the rocking of the 9000-ton ship made more than half of the 600 people sick. Dad, Mom and Yutta were also sick and had to retreat to their cabin. I finished my dessert and went to look for them.

Dad and Mom did not recover fully until we entered the St. Lawrence River.

*From Quebec we had a train ride to Calgary and Edmonton, with a stop in Winnipeg, Manitoba, to meet the Baptist officer and immigration organizer for the Baptist's "Sturhan."

*After arriving in Edmonton, we had a one-night layover at the immigration hall behind the present CN Tower. We arrived in Valleyview and stayed with the Jake Lehman family until Dad rented a house in town.

*We moved the old church in town and that was very interesting for me. I met Bill Preuss, who was the mechanic for the SSC Corp., was their cook and they took me along to Beaverlodge and to the camp. I was hoping to start as a mechanic's helper but I had to start in the kitchen. About

10 days later, one crew had to go out from the main camp for four to six days with eight to ten men and I ended up being their cook. This was out of tents and with three camp cookers resting on small tree branches nailed onto larger trees with a canopy above. This included breakfast, lunch in paper bags and dinner in the evening. And the eggs had to be perfect. If the yellow ran out, it went into the bush.

*On the second month out, the truck driver was going for supplies to Grande Prairie and asked me if I would like a driver's license. This was new and interesting to get a license without going along. All I had to do was give him my personal information and $3. I also bought a wringer washer through Marshall Wells for Mom and Dad.

*I stayed about seven months through the winter and had also bought a lot from the Adolphsons for $350. Mom and Dad built a house on it. Now I had a $3 driver's license and a $350 lot but I still wanted to go as a plumber. But I could not get a job in Edmonton on my first trip out. So I had to work for Dick Strazer for a while, mixing cement for the oil rigs.

*On another trip to Edmonton, I was promised a job in a month's time with Economy Plumbing. In the meantime, I worked on forming basements for houses, which was with the same company, Alldrite Construction. But once I got on as a plumber, it took off fast and I did the first four houses in Camble

Town, which later became Sherwood Park. Later I was more involved in commercial jobs, like Leduc's new hospital, Deer Homes in Red Deer, Tuktoyaktuk, pilot test plant, Peace River jail and W. P. Wagner High School.

I also did Stan Alldrite's personal home. But after about six years with the company, I was in the office as the second estimator. After 14 years with Economy, I decided to venture out on my own. I had also built three houses on the side. In the meantime, Mr. Alldrite wanted me to take over the commercial plumbing division, but I had to tell him that I had other plans. Then he asked me to find a replacement to run the commercial end. I interviewed three men and found my replacement so that I could take over Larry Neumann Plumbing, which I had made arrangements to purchase. (On my first trip to Edmonton, he would not give me the job. Neumann Plumbing '69 Ltd. was then the new name and two plumbers came with it, doing mainly service work. Later we purchased more trucks and went up to 14 men during the peak times. I was also a partner in building five warehouses and retired in 1995.

*After marrying Helma Adams in 1958, we had our first house in 1959, our second on 1961 and then the third in 1972. Our kids remember the third house the most as we spent 11 years there. We moved to Riverbend in 1972 for nine years and in a larger house for 15 years. Brenda and Sharon still were here for a while, and then we moved into our small house at our present address, where we have been almost 15 years.

Diane Agnes (Klumbies) Hinz (b. Dec. 13, 1959

*Diane Agnes Klumbies (b. Dec. 13, 1959) married Reinhart (Ron) Hinz on September 8, 1977. Ron incorporated Delnor Construction Ltd. with his business partner in June 1983. Delnor specializes in commercial buildings and renovations, health care and multi-family housing.

*Based on revenues, Delnor Construction currently ranks 26 among Canadian Contractors.

*Our three daughters are: Leanne Chelsey (b. Sept. 26, 1984), Jennifer Larissa (b. June 19, 1986) and Candace Danae (b. Sept. 18, 1989).

*All three daughters were born in Edmonton and have given us so much joy throughout the years. The girls played volleyball for several years along with some coaching after high school.

*Our family went on many camping trips in the summers and boating and water sports were enjoyed from the time the girls were born. We spent most years in Sherwood Park and still live there today.

Leanne (Hinz) Austring (b. Sept. 26, 1984

*Upon high school graduation, Leanne went to Oahu, Hawaii, for five months beginning in January 2003 to attend Youth with a Mission (YWAM) discipleship training school. Two an a half of the five months were on the mission field in Tonga and Western Samoa.

*Leanne's post-secondary schooling is a Bachelor of Commerce from the University of Alberta; she graduated in April 2007.

*Leanne married Kaylan Christopher Wayne Austring (b. Apr. 20, 1983) on May 21, 2007, on the island of Oahu in Hawaii.

*Kaylan's work background is carpentry. He was employed as a finisher for a few years then moved on to having his own framing company for a couple of years. He then shut down his business to go work at Delnor Corporation as a superintendent, which he is currently doing.

*Leanne and Kaylan's home church is Heartland Alliance Church in Sherwood Park, Alberta. Through a church partnership with Food for the Hungry in Peru, Kaylan and Leanne went on a mission trip to Greater Lima, Peru (specifically a neighbourhood called Santa Barbara) for two weeks in November 2008. Kaylan and Leanne are currently on course to return to Peru at the end of March 2011 and will be leading the team at that time.

Jennifer (Hinz) Engelman (b. June 19, 1986)

*Jennifer's post-secondary schooling is a Bachelor of Science in Nursing from the University of Alberta in Edmonton, Alberta. She works as a registered nurse in Edmonton.

*Jennifer married Daniel Terrance Bernard Engleman (b. Jan. 11, 1986) on November 13, 2010. Daniel's post-secondary schooling is a Bachelor of Arts with a History major from the University of Alberta. He owns and operates Engelman Construction Ltd., which is an Edmonton-based custom home builder.

*

Candace Hinz (b. Sept. 18, 1989)

*Candace graduated from Northern Alberta Institute of Technology with a marketing diploma. She presently lives with her parents.

Yutta (Klumbies) Adolphson (b. Jan. 20, 1940)

*I was born in East Germany close to the Lithuanian border. I have one brother, Kurt, who is five years older.

*Later we moved to a town close to Berlin. My father was in the German army by that time and I really did not get to know him until after the war.

*I was told when he did come home on furlough that I called him "Uncle" and made strange. Since we lived close to Berlin, there were planes flying over to bomb Berlin—that is something I can remember quite well. The Russians gathered up young healthy women to work for them and my mother was one of them. Somehow, I knew when she would be coming home and I always looked up the street to see if she was coming, worried that she might not return. The Russians would come into our house to find food such as fresh eggs. One of these soldiers could speak German and told us they did not want do do this but they had to survive.

*Dad had a good job in the army. He was a personal valet for his superior. After the war, Dad went to work for the same man on his farm in West Germany.

*For us to get to the West, Mom had to get a pass from the Russians for the three of us. There was one young mother with a baby who did not get her pass, so my mother handed over her pass and then she hid under a bunch of luggage until we were across the border. If the Russians would have discovered her, we would have lost our mother.

*We went to the farm where Dad worked. There I learned to ride a bicycle and I started school, which was a 4 to 5 kilometer walk. To go to church, we had to walk a long way to catch a streetcar therefore, we did not go very often.

*The last place we lived in Germany was Dusseldorf along the Rhine River. We lived quite close to the river and that is where I learned to swim.

Dad drove a truck for a brick factory. His boss had three daughters and the two younger ones became good friends of mine. We never owned a house or a car but Dad's boss had a car—a Mercedes 300—and I got to ride in it a couple of times. It was quite a thrill!

*In 1954, it was decided that we would move to Canada. Just in case Canada did not have some of these finer things of life, Mom brought a sewing machine and a set of china. The boat ride was terrible; I was sick most of the way. We landed in Quebec City and then took the train to Edmonton and then to High Prairie where we were picked up by car and taken to Valleyview. There we stayed with the Jake Lehman family. Saturday, was shopping day in town and I was told there would be Indians there. When we were in town I could not see any Indians and found out they dressed just like us and did net wear feathers on their heads or have their faces painted like I had read about. I was rather disappointed.

*I should have been in grade 9 but because I did not know the language, I went back to grade 8. Going to school and not knowing the language is quite an experience. Kids would smile at me and I thought they were laughing at me because I had braids. I found out soon that people here were much friendlier than in Germany. Since I was the only one with braids, they were soon cut off. Papa Klumbies was not too happy about his little girl having no more braids.

*After living in town for a little while and with my language improving, I was able to work and did light housework for the district nurse. One day I walked in and there was this man lying on the couch, his face swollen. I was then told it was Norm Adolphson and he had been in an explosion. I had seen Norm before—everybody knew everybody—but he sure didn't look like I had remembered him! I never thought that someday he would be my husband.

*For a little while I worked for the local barber, cleaning his shop and then waited tables at a cafe. After that I worked at Frohberger's General Store where they sold everything from soup to nuts. During that time, Norm and I started dating. We were married in 1958. We have three daughters: Rhonda, Lorraine and Sonia, and six grandchildren. And maybe someday even some great-grandchildren. My life has been good and God has been faithful. Our children's stories are included in the Adolphson stories.

Missing Family

FOUND SOME MISSING FAMILY in Norway and Germany,

In June of this year 2011 Erik Wilhehnsen informed me that he found relatives of aunt Tordis and Even Stenberg. Erik and Ruth had visited the family of Ove and Gerd Sonja Stenberg. Ove died several years ago. Gerd Sonja (84) and their son Willy were home. Tordis' daughter Else is also living in Drammen and they are planning a visit shortly.

Another daughter of Tordis', Marry Elinor, got married in Germany. She has four children and extended family, all living in Germany. Some of the family do not speak English so it might be better to have an English and Norwegian version of the story, but I can't wait any longer so we will do this project at a later date when all the information is in and get a more thorough job of assembling the information and distributing it. I have had the manuscript with the publisher who has been doing other details as well as waiting for other information over two months ago, I am being pressured to get on with the publishing. This is somewhat dissapointing but I think it will be better in the end.

Oscar & Ellen Adolphson Norman & Yutta Adolphson Madeline & Bill Klumbies wedding
Oct 25, 1958

50th wedding anniversary October 25, 1958

Rhonda & Stan Reimer Mandy
Angela—oldest Winnipeg, Manitoba

Lorraine Clair and her daughter, Stephanie Port Moody, B.C.

Norman & Yutta Rhonda Reimer—oldest Lorraine Clair—middle Sonia—youngest

Sonia and Richard Ens Carissa—12 yrs Joshua—17 yrs Damon—15 Grande Prairie, Ab.

Wedding of Jonathan and Angela Reimer Dec 27/09 Winnipeg

L-R Jack & Lois Effirds, Roy & Lila Harback, Yutta?? Adolphson, Ed & Deane Kisser, Jack & Lois Chatwin, Arnold & Dorothy Kruger, Henry & Hulda Perron, Arthur & May Joy Adolphson, Kurt & Helma Klumbies. All the above were married in 1958. Pictures taken Norm & Yutta's celebration.

Lone Tjustrup, Karen Tjustrup, Toni Adolphson, Lorraine Adolphson, Bonalyn Hennig, Alice Hennig About 1982

Norm & Yutta, Janet, Alice & Ken, Arthur & May Joy, seated Ellen, Mom, Ellen Adolphson. Family get together.

Norm, Ed Pedersen, Art, Alice Hennig, Janet Maelnes

Public Service Award

Art & Norm standing—Janet Andrew Erik Wilhelmsen & Alice Hennig Eric's frist visit about 1980

Erik & Elisabeth visit in 2008

Uncle's George & Bill Pedersen visit 1995

Yutta and I used the computor a lot for E mails and scaning photos and reduced to a 3" x 5" picture. Some of the older photo didn't turn out and others did especially if printed on photo paper.

Rhonda, Deanna, Norm, Dean & Lorraine Adolphson skiing in Jasper 1975

Alice, Arthur, Nonnan & Peter our dog

Trucks I used at my John Deere Dealership from 1958-62

Yutta, Rhonda and the name of the business—Valleyview Farm Supplies

Norm and Sam (dog)—1/2 St. Bernard & 1/2 Siberan Husky. He was trained to pull the children on a tobbagan

5 - 10

Lorraine, Sonia & Barrey 1976

Norm & Barney

7 - 10

Blaine & Bonalin Hennig enjoying the pups

The first of 3 litters of pups. The girl sold them for spending money

Angela Reimer and Grandpa 1976

Sitone mowing farm yard 1976

Playouse (traper's cabin) under construction built by their grandpa 2000

12-10

Not recommended! Near Banff Park 1965

A yearling moose take a dandylion leaf

13-16

Restored John Deere Model 60 Tractor. Trailer build especially for equipment installed on it. IHC Grant Grinder—J.D.—6HP Engine - Cord wood Buzz Saw in original configuration. Used in Valleyview area by Ivor Bertland. Norm Adolphson did all the building and the restoring. Unit in the Valleyview Parade—1997

14-10

Root Picker I designed and fabricated for windowing root & tree stumps as well as large rocks. It work very well. It was built where it is located in yard. Front caster wheels allow the machine to follow land contours better. Also wheel for transporting end-wise on the road 1966

Combing wheat on Dec. 27/85. We had 1½ ft of snow and a "Chinook" melted the snow except some drifts on the side hills. The grain was dried in Jan.

John Deere 8' Power Binder owned by Art Adolphson. Richard Ens on tractor. Norm Adolphson on binder. Damon on tractor riding. Field of wheat donated to the Canadian Food Grains Bank for distribution to needy countries. About 5 combines donated by their owners to harvest on Gerald Finsters alnd. Tractor restored John Deere Model 60 Std

Threshing wheat as was done in the past until the early 1950's. Thresting machine tractor & truck owned by Art Adolphson

Norman Adolphson

I was the first born in our family, on July 1, 1935, in High Prairie, Alberta, about 95 km northeast of Valleyview. That was the closest hospital to Valleyview at that time. We lived on a farm on which the larger part of Valleyview was located. One of the highlights of my early childhood was a trip to Edmonton in 1939 to observe the King and Queen's visit. I remember leaving Art to be cared for by Bertha Pettersson and crossing the Athabaska River on the ferry. I was not happy when Dad had to drive up the hill away from the ferry so far but we were not allowed to ride in the vehicle while on the ferry., The only thing I remember about the royal visit was all the soldiers marching and the soldier beat on a base drum.

My earliest memory was the day Art was born, which I have described earlier. I was not quite three years old.

My first day in school stands out. Mary Werklund was my first teacher. She taught grades one to eight in a log school that had little or no insulation. She printed our names on our desks and gave us some coloring to do and then assigned older students to work with us occasionally. I had about 1 ¾ miles to walk to and from school. There were about 46 students.

World War II was being fought and most of the young men of the area were in the army. Dad needed help with tractor driving and he would put me, at seven years old, harrowing on the tractor while he was close at hand to observe. I had no problems. The next year I pulled the binder with the tractor and then started plowing.

Dad started a re-building program in 1941. He built a new garage, pump house, barn, cow sheds and corrals. In 1947 the house was built and I helped with concrete work, stuccoing, plastering, hauling in top soil and shingling the roof. That fall, Art and I cut a lot of the crop. Art drove the tractor and I operated the binder. Andrew Rusten did most of the stooking. Dad paid us by the day so we had some spending money and he let us use the little Ford tractor for transportation.

I also took a contract to clean schools, light the fires in the stoves and oil the floors three times a year. I would share this with three girls my age and they would each sweep one room every day.

I also had the contract to light fires and clean the waiting room and pebble the ice in the first two-sheet curling rink. I did these jobs until 1952 when I graduated from Grade 10, which was as far as a person could go for schooling in Valleyview at that time. I was also president of the students' union for two or three years.

I got a job for about 1 ½ months building the "chicken coop" school, working with Kalmer Ramstad, Ingvald Lingstad, John Ramstad and Norman Ramstad during July and August. I later took my grade 10 in that same school which was a one room building.

I wanted to be a farmer so went to agricultural school in Fairview, Alberta, where I graduated with honors in the spring of 1954. I then bought a quarter of land from Dad and also rented a quarter and did reasonably well. I homesteaded a half section of land when I was 18 years old.

In 1955, Dad acquired the John Deer dealership and operated that for two years. During that time, I rented his farm and machinery but also helped him with the ordering of parts and machinery, as well as setting up of machines. We also helped build the new shop building in 1955. We used lumber, from timber we sawed with our own sawmill. This was a family operation. We used horses for skidding logs and later used the tractor or crawler. I did most of the sawing of the lumber for all the new buildings that were built in later years. We also used wood to fuel our stoves. Dad hired a saw mill to cut lumber before that time.

Dad and I switched roles again in 1958 and I took over the business while he ran the farm and rented my portion of it.

Yutta and I were married October 25, 1958, and we moved into a small home that I acquired next to the business. When Rhonda was born in 1959, we moved into Dads house (which was equipped with water and sewer) in town.

The business did well and we were able to make ends meet. I enjoyed setting up machinery and meeting new people. I was selling from Debolt to Sunset House, Whitemud, Guy and sometimes as far as High Prairie. I needed a good banker, which I had, but the pressure was tremendous—especially if there was bad fall weather or poor prices. I had to pay my parts account at the month's end so I really needed more capital of my own.

About this time, I had the opportunity to take the Grande Prairie dealership over and received an offer of capitalization from John Deere. I decided against this and went into farming instead.

I sold a #50 John Deere Backhoe to Don Dixon which we mounted on a John Deere 420 crawler equipped with a dozer blade. He operated this for a year or two and he traded it in on some farm machinery. My brother Art and I formed a partnership and we bought this unit. Art was the main operator at first. It was the third one manufactured. We worked in the oilfield, for farmers and the town of Valleyview. The backhoe was detachable so it was a very versatile machine. We had this for about three years. The business was growing and became incompatible with our farming operations so we sold it to Norman Ramstad, who had been our operator for some time.

It was during this time that Dad and I again changed roles. He retired to the house in Valleyview and I bought his building site and the adjoining fraction along the river. Lorraine and Sonia were born after we moved to the farm. In 1961, I sold the business to Elmer Chugg, and he operated it for about two years.

I bought several fractions and quarter sections of raw land while we were connected and cleared about 700 acres with a brush cutter and piler and burned the windrows of brush and trees. Some of it was "broken" (plowed) with a one-bottom plow with a farm tractor fitted with steel wheels with six-inch steel lugs and a one bottom 20 inch breaking plow. The balance was cleared and broken with a D8 caterpillar and a four-bottom plow, with 24 inch cutting width each.

To remove the roots, I built a side-delivery root picker that cut a swath of 10 feet. It was driven by power take-off by a John Deere 820 diesel tractor. While I was building it, Don Penson bought a fifty percent share in the m machine and helped build it. It took 25 days and we hired Don Dixon to help us. Dick Hollingworth and his father bought it from us after we were done with it.

The Little Smoky River wound its way through the farm. It was somewhat of a barrier for getting machinery back and forth. However, it also served as a recreation area. We had a sandbar near home where we would swim. It was quite safe because there were no "holes" and the water was slow-moving. We and our friends had a lot of good times there. It was also great to snowmobile on in the winter—we could go for miles. We also followed seismic trails in the bush and would cook coffee around a campfire. We had a Honda trike. The whole family would use it and the two snowmobiles for recreational use. I used them for tasks on the farms as well.

We sold the farm in 1994 and had an auction sale. The farm was sold to Robert Lehman who died suddenly and is being actively farmed by his widow Katrine.

The girls mention in their stories about the St. Bernard dogs and pups and raising pigs. The dogs would always follow the kids to wherever they played and would even stop them if they weren't getting along.

We bought a four level split house in Valleyview and lived there for 13 years and sold it and bought a condominium in the Shepherds's Village and moved here in May 2007 and are here presently (2011).

I have been active in community activities most of my life. I helped organize the Valleyview Seed Cleaning Co-op and served on the board of directors, served on the agricultural service board and helped acquire the community grazing lease, was a delegate for United Farmers of Alberta (UFA) for many years, was a delegate for two terms with Alberta Wheat pool, was a trustee for East Smoky School Division for 16 ½ years, served as mayor of Valleyview for twelve years and am a member of the Emmanuel Baptist Church.

I have had problems with my health, had a pace maker and three stints installed in my heart. Last year I had major back surgery which included opening 3 lumbars and freeing nerves and removal of two discs which included opening lumbars and fusing the lumbars together again to my pelvis. This operation was successful but I need to be careful.

As a member of Emmanuel Baptist Church, I was involved in many activities of the church, including moderator and trustee. I served six out of seven years as the building board chairman, during which time the new church was built. It was my job to act as general contractor and hire and supervise all the trades we had hired to do the various tasks. There was a great deal of donated labor as well, which reduced the cost of the church building substantially.

I want to tell you just a bit about my faith in God and Jesus Christ. I believe Jesus Christ is who He says He is!

In the Christmas story as recorded in the Holy Bible, it gives several instances where Christ fulfilled prophecy concerning His coming into the world as a baby, ministering to the Jewish and non-Jewish people, performing miracles, being wrongly judged, being killed on the cross, rising from the dead and ascending into Heaven. There are many witnesses to these events. It would not be possible for Him to be an imposter because He had no control over the events that were going to happen to Him later, including how He would die. He came to life again on the third day and later ascended to heaven and there were many witnesses to these events.

The historian Flavius Josephus, who lived at that time, described Him as supernatural.

He was born as a lowly peasant from poor people and had no one to promote Him except for John the Baptist, who was thought of by many as a "nut case" because he wore animal skins and ate honey and grasshoppers and lived in the wilderness. He was prophesied to come on the scene and he attracted large crowds in the rural areas and pointed the way to Christ as being the Messiah as promised to the Jews and Gentiles.

Those researching the Bible's accuracy from an historical perspective as well as archaeological, found that local traditions and ancient writings confirm its accuracy.

The Bible is the only book of major religions that contains prophetic scriptures from beginning to end, many of which have been fulfilled. An example of that is the rebirth of Israel after 2500 years in which they also revived their original language.

Creation's another example of God's existence. It is all around us in nature. Every species regenerates its own kind and they have specific purposes and sometimes depend on other species for their survival. Scientific discoveries, properly applied, confirm this. If there is a design, there must be a designer.

If, for some reason, a person is called to move to a foreign country to live, they usually investigate what is required of them to make the move and what the circumstances are in which they will find themselves when they get there. The same thing applies to us when we die. It seems logical to find out for ourselves what is going to happen to our souls after we die and if we have choices. This is our responsibility. The Bible says: The fool says in his heart; "There is no God." Psalm 53:1.

Rhonda Elaine (Adolphson) Reimer (b. June 16. 1959)

When my children were young and into playing their very tragic imaginary version of "Little House on the Prairie," they would frequently bemoan the fact that they didn't live on a farm. According to them, it just wasn't fair that both Stan and I grew up on a farm and they had to live in the city. Well, farm life hasn't been our choice as adults, but I have to agree that there were a lot of fun things as kids about life in the country. Especially because we were not "too far" in the country . . . not too far from town, with still lots of room for our toys and activities. I especially liked being close enough to neighboring kids to get together independently of our parents. In the winter we often travelled across country by snowmobile to Hufnagel's, Finster's, Lehman's, Uncle Art's—and closer by, to the Johnson's. We all had snowmobiles and had great fun with them. We also enjoyed playing games, especially on our longer breaks from school. I recall Monopoly games with the Lehman boys or Dean and Deanna that went on for days. Of course, there was also farm work—not so enjoyable. Living close to the river, we usually had to pick rocks and roots in the summer. Of course we were paid, which was motivation, but just as motivating was the "great tan" we'd get, which began with a good sunburn as it was achieved without the use of sunscreen. We were so uninformed in those days! Looking back, I wonder what Uncle Andrew thought of us and our silly teenage chatter while we worked.

And the St. Bernard dogs—we enjoyed them a lot, especially when they were puppies. As adults they were occasionally very annoying. I remember Lorraine and I setting up a tent close to the granaries to camp outside. We had gone to town to get snacks (we had just discovered yogurt and that was a favorite snack) and were sitting in the tent chatting and eating. I don't remember if it was Sandy or Barney, but one of the dogs was with us. When we went to sleep, we kicked the dog out. But not to worry, she or he would protect us. It slept right outside the tent flap all night, snoring very loudly. It wasn't a good night's sleep for us. These dogs also weren't too much fun when we were trying to get a suntan. Seeing someone prone on the ground triggered their rescue instinct and they would try to "save" us. After all, we were lying motionless on the ground; therefore, we needed to be revived. This was done by lying half on top of us and half beside us to warm us up! Their rescue instinct also applied to moving objects such as toboggans and snowmobiles. We were pulled off of them as it was obviously too dangerous. And for some reason, Sandy didn't like it when we got on the school bus either.

On December 20, 1980, I married Stan Reimer (b. May 16, 1958) from Wawanesa, Manitoba. We met at Winnipeg Bible College (now Providence College). Stan continued his studies there, graduating in 1983. I attended Red River College where I took a bookkeeping course and finished in 1981. I worked as a bookkeeper until Angela Camille (b. Sept. 13, 1983) was born. Stan drove long distance for a couple years and then went back to school to get his Bachelor of Education. During this time, Amanda Renee (b. Nov. 20, 1985) was born. Stan graduated in 1988 and he and Angela "started school" the same fall—Angela in Kindergarten and Stan teaching junior high in New Bothwell, Manitoba. After nine years of teaching, Stan obtained his MCSE (Microsoft Certified Systems Engineer) and taught for a local technical college. He had a few other positions, eventually starting his own company in 2003. I spent ten years working for Mennonite Central Committee, most of those with the Canada division. I started out as an administrative assistant and moved to director of administrative services. It is an organization that I respect greatly and personally support as much as I can.

Well, now I have two adult daughters. After Angela graduated from high school, she went to the University of Winnipeg for a year and to Providence College for one year. Then she decided to go overseas, to Arusha, Tanzania, with the Mennonite Central Committee as a SALTer (serve and learn together). She lived with a Tanzanian family and worked in a nursery school. She became very fluent in Swahili. One of the highlights of that year was a family vacation we took to Tanzania. We so appreciated Angela's ability to speak the local language as so much had to be bartered. We went on a safari in the Serengeti and saw zebras, wildebeest, cheetahs, giraffes, elephants, rhinoceroses, lions and the elusive leopard (pronounced lee-oh-pard by our guide). We spent four wonderful days on the island of Zanzibar—such a beautiful and historic place. When Angela returned from Tanzania, she enrolled in Education at the University of Manitoba, specializing in early years. Now she is a kindergarten teacher. She married Jonathan Klassen (b. April 23, 1983) on December 27,2009. She and Jonathan were good friends from ages four to seven or so when we lived on the same street and attended the same church. The Klassens moved away, eventually returning to Winnipeg. However, it wasn't until fall of 2007 that they reconnected on Facebook. Jonathan is working on a B.A. in History from the University of Winnipeg and is delivering mail for Canada Post.

After Amanda graduated from high school, she too attended Providence College for one year. She graduated form the University of Manitoba with a Bachelor of Arts (Hon) in Psychology. She then moved to Edmonton to attend the University of Alberta to earn and M.Sc. in Speech Language Pathology. She completed her training in July 2010 and is actively looking for a job in Manitoba. Amanda is our horse girl. She currently owns two horses, nicknamed, "Old" and "Lame". The girls worked many hours of babysitting and at McDonald's to buy Rocket ("Old") when they were in junior high. Armada continues to take riding lessons and leases a third horse that she uses to enter local equestrian competitions.

Stan and I started our own company, S.R. Technical Services, in April 2003. Stan is the technical guru here and I am the administrative guru. We provide technical writing and consulting services. Our biggest customer is Microsoft Learning, for whom we develop and write courseware.

In October 2005 we purchased a small cottage at Big Whiteshell Lake in Whiteshell Provincial Park. This is in the Canadian Shield about two hours east of Winnipeg. Stan is able to work there with satellite internet and we spend as much time there as we can in the months between May and September. The view is spectacular and we enjoy being there very much.

And I just want to add here that it was NOT me that instigated the skinny-dipping with the Chugg girls. It must have been Sonia. Lorraine's memory is somewhat lacking.

Lorraine Ann (Adolphson) Clair (b. Dec. 26. 1961)

Lorraine's birthday is December 26, which usually meant that there was a big family gathering (and more presents!!) while she was growing up. Later on it meant Boxing Day sales! Maybe that is why she loves shopping so much.

She was the "boy" in the family. She would rather go out and work in the yard than stay in the house and clean. She enjoyed helping Dad fix the machinery by handing him the tools. She always wanted to milk the cows but the one "Bossy" milk cow we had was hard to milk. When she was about 10, the cows were all sold.

Later, in her early teens, Lorraine got into the business of raising pigs that Dad bought for her as wieners. The deal was that if she raised them, Dad would sell one of them and give her the money while the other one would be butchered for family dinners. She raised two pairs of wiener pigs and they became her pets. She spent hours at the barn playing with them. When the pigs got older they were too big to crawl onto her lap but they still tried—and those hard hooves left her knees in a state of perpetual bruises.

She seemed okay with the arrangement of selling one pig for the money and was not outwardly remorseful about the situation. To this day, however, she does not enjoy pork.

There were three things about living at the farm that Lorraine especially liked. The first was that they had a huge dog. They had a few St. Bernard pups growing up and even raised a couple of litters. The look on people's faces when they would lay eyes on the dog was always priceless. The first one, Sandy, was very protective and would follow them everywhere to guard them. There friends dared not even play rough as she would bark and give them a good scare. She never ever hurt anyone, however. It was only her size that was intimidating. Barney, the next dog, wanted to keep them at home and would hold onto the back of their coats as they tried to get on the school bus. One of the girls would have to plug his nostrils until he let go and they could board.

Another thing that Lorraine really enjoyed was the swimming hole in the river. It was always fun when a bunch of people would come down and they would go swimming and roast hotdogs and marshmallows. They would get to ride in the back of the pick-up truck down the side of the field—a travel arrangement usually reserved for only the dog. Once, when Lorraine was about 15, the Chugg girls joined Rhonda and her skinny-dipping venture at the river. By that time they were old enough to drive themselves and were confident that no one would see them. But suddenly, while they swam, they heard shouting. There on the other side of the river's shore were both sets of parents! They had gone on a tour of the farm and happened to end up on the other side of the swimming hole. Luckily, they did not notice the naked state—or at least pretended not to notice. (If anyone asks, it was Rhonda's idea).

Lastly, the part of the farm life that Lorraine really loved was the snowmobiling. She spent her high school years out on the fields on a John Deere 300 or 440. From the time school ended to when it got dark, she, Melody Johnson and David Hufnagel would be driving all over—Suicide Hill was a favorite destination, as was the Finster's, the Lehman's and the Penner's. Life could have been simpler for her parents had she had a cell phone back then—there were a few times when she got stuck in a remote area and had to walk a few miles to get help. Despite a few negative experiences, Lorraine still loves snowmobiling and had had many chances to enjoy the sport in the mountains around Vancouver, where she now lives.

Lorraine was a good student in school and graduated with good marks. She knew she wanted to be a school teacher in Grade 9 when, upon fainting after getting a needle at school, she knew "nurse" was no longer a valid option. And of course, being a teacher was the only other one that was really ever discussed. No regrets. Ever.

Note: Lorraine met the love of her life and is being married December 20, 2011; the same date that her two sisters had chosen earlier as their wedding dates.

And so, she focused on biology as she loved to dissect things—when she went fishing with family friends, it was Robert Lehman and she who would clean (or should I say "dissect") the fish and bring them back to the others.

In university, she chose biology and home economics as her major specialties as a teacher. Ironically, it has always been her home economics which has gotten her hired; first in Valleyview and later in Viking, Alberta, and Burnaby, British Columbia.

She had a variety of jobs over the four year period she attended university, such as paving, road construction, government road maintenance and restaurant cooking—the first of which was for Ken and Alice Hennig's Drive-in in Valleyview.

In her second year of university, Lorraine got married to a preacher's son. That only lasted two years, however. She decided to keep the name as it was easy to pronounce and the students had already come to know her as Mrs. Clair. She goes by that name to this day.

After university, Lorraine came back to Valleyview and taught at Hillside High School for seven years. It was interesting getting to know her old teachers as colleagues. She especially enjoyed being the student council advisor and planning many zany events that helped to keep the school spirit alive.

Later, Lorraine moved to Viking, Alberta where she taught for three years. She got to know some of the Sutter family who had several sons playing in the NHL.

In 1986, Lorraine was in a relationship that brought a lovely daughter, Stefanie Broad (b. May 12, 1986), into her life. Stef has grown up to be a beautiful, kind-hearted, intelligent and humorous young lady and is presently going to Kwantlen University in Metro, Vancouver, specializing in the business field. And she loves animals as much as her mother does. In fact, she presently works at a wildlife rescue center, where trumpeter swans, raccoons and pigeons have replaced her former pet loves—bearded dragons, snakes, hamsters and frogs—of her youth.

When Stef was going into Grade 2, the family moved to the Vancouver area and Lorraine started teaching high school in Burnaby. Both of them love the West Coast lifestyle ~ especially the great outdoors and the beautiful coastal mountains. After a few years of hard work, Lorraine received her Master's degree from San Diego State University. She presently works in a leadership position at a new high school that she helped to open. She also runs a catering business with a group of students as part of her job. Yutta's influence of great cooking has come in handy. She looked forward to retirement in the next decade or so, and when she is not traveling, will enjoy her time in her home overlooking the ocean

Sonia Fay (Adolphson) Ens (b. Dec. 8. 1966)

My first memories are of the farm on the Little Smoky River. I remember getting lost following the St. Bernard, falling through the snow in the bush and Great Uncle Andrew's coming to my rescue. I have lots of memories of church and family gatherings. There are great memories of Bible camp, youth group activities, and especially the times when the youth group gathered at our home. We went on camping trips to B. C. with the Harback and Lehman families. On one such trip, we left Brad behind accidentally at one of our stops and had to go back to retrieve him.

The dog would carry my books or shoes while I would walk to the bus. I played with Victoria Johnson and the Hess twins as we were all neighbors. We played and jumped out of the hay loft and played "drive-in" in the playhouse. We went tubing behind the snowmobile with family and friends and I loved horseback riding with Corinne and Brian Reicher.

I took band in elementary and high school, which allowed me to do lots of traveling, including a trip to California where our band had been invited to perform and compete in an international band festival. I also took figure skating for several years. During that time, I also had a horse, loved to snowmobile with friends and family and always loved the family gatherings at Christmas at our farm.

After high school I started college in Grande Prairie to get my hairstylist license and then transferred to Winnipeg to complete it. I lived with Rhonda and her family while I was in college. When I completed the college part of my training, I shared a basement suit with my friend Gloria and started working in a salon as an apprentice hairstylist. I worked in Winnipeg for a year and then moved back to Alberta, where I met and married Richard Ens (b. Dec. 28, 1964) on December 20, 1986. I worked in various salons until 1992 when I decided to open a salon in our home. Richard and I had the first of three children in May 1991. Joshua Richard (b. May 28, 1991) was a long-awaited arrival. Damon Christopher (b. Nov. 28, 1993) came next, and our daughter Carissa (b. Oct. 4, 1996) rounded out our family. Richard went to college to get his journeyman welder's certificate in 2002 and I added school board trustee to my career around the same time.

We have resided on our acreage since 1988, building a new, larger house there in 2002. We have now decided to move from Debolt to Grande Prairie and sold our property and have built a new home.

A note from Dad:

When Sonia was small, she was a loner because Rhonda and Lorraine are seven and a half and five years older than she, so they didn't have much in common. Sonia learned to entertain herself using the Childcraft books for ideas as well as her own imagination. Before she started school, she built a tent trailer out of light cardboard paper and glue and it just looked great. She made it for her barbie dolls. It was well proportioned and fairly sturdy.

The three girls are now great friends and phone one another often, which we like to see.

Arthur & May Joy Adolphson. 1958

Arthur, May Joy Adolphson and Arthur's mother, Ellen Adolphson
on Dempster Highway in the Yukon-1993

Arthur & Bud

Back Row
Caleb Romano, Avery Romano, Danna Adolphson, Art Adolphson, Tate Adolphson, May Jay Adolphson

Middle Row
Brittany Fitzmaurice, Tyler Smith, Bob Romano, Helden Adolphson, Tomi Pomano, John Myciak, Kathy Adolphson, Deanna Fitzmaurice, Dana Adolphson, Debbie Adolphson, Dean Adolphson

Front Row
Chelsea & Calleigh Y Shawn Stepien, Kieth Adolphson, Sarah Adolphson, Cassidy Adolphson, Marla Maye, Ryan Myciab, Gerad Mayer

Dean Adolphson with his family

Dean & Debbie Adolphson, Danna, Sarah, Marla and Gerald Mayer

Shawn Stapier, Chelsea, Calleigh, Tyler Smith, Brittany and Deanna Fitzmearice

Caleb, Avery, Bob, Paige and Toni Romano

John Myciak, Kathy & Ryan

Keith, Tate, Cassidy and Hellene Adolphson

Chelsea, Deanna & Brittany Fitzmaurice

Sarah & Dale Hepfner wedding in Edmonton Dec. 2009

Arthur Adolphson

(from Norm's version)

Arthur Wesley Adolphson was born March 17, 1927, at home in Valleyview. The district nurse assisted with the birth.

I (Norm) remember all the hustle in the house and later my dad showed me the baby and they put him in my crib. I didn't like that! That was probably the beginning of the rivalry.

When Arthur was about 13, he got sick with nythritus, a fatal kidney disease at that time for children and adults. Because he was 13, there was a chance he could outgrow the disease, but it required special care. He was in bed at home from April until the fall under the care of our district nurse Gwen Goodin. He recovered from that and he has lived a reasonably healthy life. That was a tough summer for our mother and him!

Our Dad also held me responsible for looking after Art. If he got in trouble, I (Norm) got in trouble for not watching him closely enough.

Art had a small John Deere 40 tractor with a dozer on it that he used to work with oil companies and farmers as well as the town of Valleyview. Later he and I (Norm) had a small J-D crawler with a back hoe mounted on it, and we worked throughout the Valleyview area.

At about the same time he bought the land he presently lives on, as well as other land and started farming, which he is still doing. However, he has reduced the amount of acres he farms.

He married May Joy Lusch on June 15, 1958, and later moved to the present farm where he built or replaced the old buildings.

After 12 years of marriage, Art went to Alberta Vocational College in Fort McMurray, Alberta. In 1970-1971 he attended Southern Alberta Institute of Technology (SAIT) in Calgary, Alberta, achieving his second class ticket in welding.

In the 1970s he got into a high-pressure testing business, testing oil rigs, pipelines and well casings for leaks that could cause environmental damage or injure the workman who were operating equipment. He eventually sold this business and began helping his sons, Dean and Keith, with their farms.

Dean Edward Adolphson (b. April 9. 1959)

Dean was the firstborn. He graduated from Hillside High School in Valleyview and then started working in the oilfields in the area, operating heavy duty machinery and large trucks. He had a business neutralizing and cleaning oil well sites after drilling was completed.

While he was doing this he and Debbie bought a farm near town in which they specialized in raising riding horses along with cattle, grain and hay.

Dean and Deborah Lea Farrow (b. March 12, 1962, in Ontario) were married March 30, 1985. Debbie has a degree in petroleum engineering that she earned in Ontario. She and Dean met on an oil well drilling site. Besides taking an active interest in the farm, she trains and shows horses as well as competes in events in western Canada. Her daughters have also followed in their mother's footsteps in riding and competing with success. She presently serves on the board of directors of the United Farmers of Alberta Cooperative.

Marla Ashley (b. January 3, 1988) is presently working for a law firm in Peace River, Alberta, where she lives with her husband, Jared Edward Mayer (b. December 18,1986), a carpenter. Marla and Jared were married March 29, 2008.

Sarah Deanne Hepfner

Sarah Deanne (b. December 8, 1989) graduated from Hillside High School has been working in Edmonton. She was married in Mexico during the Christmas holidays in 2009. Her husband, Dale Patrick Hepfner (b. March 20, 1979) is working at house construction and in partnership in agriculture field spraying.

Dana Lea Adolphson

Dana Lea (b. January 19, 1992) graduated from Hillside High School in June 2009. She has taken a year off from schooling to help on the farm, but plans to go to college in the future. She won the Canadian championships in Regina, Saskatchewan. She also won National championship, jumping 17 hurdles with her horse in the equestrian even.

Deanna Esther (Adolphson) Fitzmaurice (b. June 7. 1960)

Deanna took her schooling in Valleyview and then acquired her teaching degree at the University of Albert. She began her teaching career in Edmonton where she is presently teaching and serves as vice-principal in her school. She lives in Sherwood Park, Alberta

Deanna married Brian Ludgar Fitzmaurice (b. February 16, 1954) on May 22, 1982. He organized and operated a successful company that serviced the tar sands area of northern Alberta. He also liked hunting and fishing and spent time around Valleyview doing so. They were divorced in 2007.

Deanna and Brian have two daughters—Chelsea and Brittany Amber.

Chelsea (b. December 10, 1982) married Shawn Edward Stepien, who is a B-pressure welder working in the Edmonton area where they reside. Chelsea is a safety trainer for Pool Construction

Ltd. (PCL). They have a daughter, Calleigh Ava, (b. March 4, 2008), who is their pride and joy. They now have a son, Carson Shawn (b. June 14, 2010).

Brittany (b. May 20, 1985) finished all her school in 2009 and is a professional writer based in Edmonton. She has her own consulting business and offers freelance writing for hospitals of northern Canada, working mostly for the Inuit people. She is working on a children's booklet about different health issues. She has also written manuals for oil companies.

Kathrvn Mae (Adolphson) Mvcek (b. May 31. 1964)

Kathryn acquired her nursing degree and began her career in Grande Prairie, Alberta. She worked in the hospital therefore 16 years. She married John Edward Mycek on November 9, 2002. They now live on a farm north of Debolt, Alberta. John received his picker ticket and was top in Alberta at NAIT in 2001.

In 2005, he started John Mycek Trucking Ltd., which he operates in the off-season in conjunction with his farm. Kathy is presently employed by Alberta Health Services in Valleyview. They have one son, Ryan Joseph Wesley (b. September 4, 2003).

Keith Randall Adolphson (b. July 28. 1968)

Keith likes the outdoors and has been an industrial machinery operator and truck operator. Presently he is a carpenter specializing in building houses.

Keith and Helene Lise France Bertrand (b. May 12, 1970 in Quebec) were married April 14, 2001. Helene came west and began working in the BC forest industry and later came to work in Alberta in the same industry. She later got involved driving large tanker trucks hauling crude oil in Valleyview. She met Keith in the local Valleyview Oilfields.

Shortly after they got married, they acquired an acreage from Arthur and May Joy, which they developed. Since then, they also acquired a goat herd that fluctuates between 300 and 500 heads. They have three distinct breeds from which they market the offsprings. They have four Akbash guard dogs, which are a special off-shore breed, running with the goats.

They have two children—Cassidy Morgan (b. January 16, 2003) and Tate Oscar Wesley (b. July 6, 2005).

Toni Ginette (Adolphson) Romano (b. February 13, 1970

Toni went to Canadian Bible College (CBC) in Regina, Saskatchewan, for one semester after finishing high school. She then went to Grande Prairie College and got two years' credit toward a teaching degree. She was involved in children's ministries in Saskatchewan, Alberta and British Columbia.

It was at this time she met up again with one of her classmates from CBC, Robert (Bob) Romano, who was the pastor of Beaverlodge Alliance Church. They were married June 15, 1991, Robert Charles Romano (b. June 4, 1964) was raised in Cranbrook, B. C. Bob was an active hockey player and played goal for the Hythe Mustangs among other teams. He has been in the ministry since. He and Toni are presently ministering at Millboume Alliance Church in Edmonton.

Toni graduated with distinction with a Bachelor of Education degree in the spring of 2009 and now has a teaching job near her home. She also has a Bachelor of Arts degree. Bob has resigned from his pastoral position and is now operating his own business, Bob's Bus Service. He takes sports teams or any other group to different events or wherever they want to go.

Toni and Bob have three children. Kaleb (b. Sept. 6, 1993) is currently in Grade 11. He has been a recipient every year since Grade 9 to different art schools. In August 2009 he received a scholarship to Red Deer College for one week—Summer Scapes. His art work consist of water, oil and acrylic paintings, paper mache, masks, clay and ceramic figurines. He has won several first prize ribbons at school and fairs. He also makes puppets and helps his mother and aunt at youth camp. He also plays the trumpet.

Avrey (b. January 9, 1996) is a sports-minded young man in Grade 9, hockey being his favourite sport. One of the teams he played with took them to Toronto, Vancouver, Calgary and Edmonton. In 2006-2007, they were second best Atom team in Alberta. Avrey is currently with the AA Knights of Columbus Voyagers. Baseball and soccer are the summer-time play. He may be small but he is mighty. If you want to know something about cars, just ask Avrey. He enjoys mechanics and woodwork as well.

Paige (b. September 4, 1999) is our gymnast and has competed in Montreal, Winnipeg, Vancouver and Calgary. In Montreal she came in fourth in her age group. She has received first place in the provincial and national's aspire category and second in western Canada for 2009, held in Winnipeg. Currently she practices 20 hours per week in preparation for the 2010 pre-novice national elite championship.

Arthur Adolphson—by himself

I entered this world March 17, 1938. What an entry it was and an exciting day! Finally, I got to meet my mother and dad and also my "big" brother Norman who was a little over two years old. I don't recall much about the fuss they made over me, but one thing I do know was that I was loved!

I'll share a few memories, highlights and events of my life as I remember it.

A few years after I was born, Alice and Janet joined the family. When Alice was about three or four, she would run away to town every now and then. Norman and I had the "privilege" of hunting her down. Sometimes we'd take her between us. One time I tied her to the clothes line—perhaps that wasn't the most popular thing to do, She wasn't really happy about that.

I made some wooden toys for us to play with. One day I found her with a hammer, smashing her toy to pieces. She said: "I'm not going to play with you anymore." I guess that was a new phase in her life—she was growing up.

I believe it was mentioned earlier when at 13 years of age I had nephritis (a kidney disease) and was laid up for some time. Not long before our mother's passing away, she told me that when she worked in the garden, hilling potatoes, she would pray many prayers for my healing. Those prayers were answered.

The day Janet was born, Dad, Norman and I were playing horseshoes. Dad went into the house to listen to the hospital bulletins on the radio. When he came back out he said: "We have a baby sister and her name is Hazel." She's been a wonderful sister. Her name was Hazel Janet. Norman and I didn't like that name and we asked our parents to call her Janet. Dad preferred Hazel because he pronounced Janet as "Yanet", but later agreed and learned to say her name properly.

After I was married, I had driven to the river to see my folks. Unbeknownst to us, Janet had gotten into my car and lay down on the floor in the back seat. When I was almost home, she made her presence known. I turned around and headed back to the folks' place. They were already down by the river looking for her.

At about age 16-17, I bought a BSA 650 Golden Flash motorcycle with 1900 miles on it. Oskar Lunder and Knut Berg, both from Norway, bought it in Halifax and drove it out west. I was short $50.00 of the funds to buy it so I asked my dad if he'd loan it to me. His reply was: "Not a chance." But Oskar and Knut loaned it to me until I got a job during the summer holidays. One day I heard it going west of town—with Alice on it. It wasn't idling either.

One summer the Rierson Circus came to Valleyview. They had two bear cubs tethered alongside the tent. After attending the regular circus events, Norman and I went to where the bears were. This was later in the afternoon. We started wrestling with them. Then I lay down and took the bear on top of me and it started to purr—well, what a noise! It sounded like a D-7 Cat. That was such an experience, one I will never forget. As well, the elephant trainers brought the elephants to my folks to give then a drink of water.

Our dad was a very practical man—not too much was wasted. If any building was torn apart, the nails were saved. In the winter he'd bring a block of wood into the house on which to straighten the nails. Spring brought new building projects.

Speaking of nails—during the earlier years, times were somewhat hard. I recall our mother making shoes for us. They had a thin leather sole on them. This is where the subject of nails comes in, literally at times! It was not the most comfortable feeling.

I have done a few foolish things in my youth. One comes to mind when Arne Johnson, Steve Lusch and I rode the ice out on the Little Smoky River one spring. I will have to admit that I was the follower and not the leader.

At the age of 31, I went to Fort McMurray to a vocational school where I started taking welding. The next winter I finished at Southern Alberta Institute of Technology (SAIT) in Edmonton and got my ticket. I worked in Pine Point, Northwest Territories the following winter. This has helped much for doing my own repairs, etc. I had planned on setting up my own business on the farm but had a hard time to charge enough.

Being away for three months at a time in the winter while I was taking this schooling and then working up north was a good stretch on my life. I met many neat people. It also gave me a new appreciation for May Joy and family.

I worked on the oil rigs, provided backhoe and cat work, drove log trucks and pressure-tested in the oilfields on rigs for 15 years. In this area, we've been blessed with the oilfield, forestry and other types of work at out "fingertips", almost at our doorstep. Some were well-paying jobs, which was good for raising a family plus supporting the farm.

I met May Joy Lusch (b. September 27, 1939) in 1954 at school and we were married June 15, 1958 (that's 52 years now!) The Baptist minister, Mr. Unrau, did the service for us at the Church of God. We had a small reception in the in-law's living room. A 1949 Mercury car was our pride and joy. We went to Wyoming for our honeymoon, where we took in a youth camp, visited May Joy's birthplace at Cody, Wyoming, met several relatives and went to Yellowstone Park.

Now in the later years of our life, we go to the Yukon, Northwest Territories and Alaska to enjoy the beautiful creation. We have been to several First Nations communities where we gave out the "Jesus" DVD and videos and have met so many wonderful people. What and experience!

In 1993, we took Mom with us; she was 83 at the time. We drove across the Arctic Circle where the Tundra is. Her reaction was "I've read about it, I've taught it and now I get to see it!"

Up to this point, we are working towards retirement. We have enjoyed living on the farm, which is about 1 1/2 miles from town. So we are nice and close to the coffee shops where we often visit with friends and family. We love the country and hope that Valleyview can always be our home. Who knows?

I have a deep appreciation and love for my parents but it seems like we didn't have them long enough, especially our Dad.

It took a real pioneer with a pioneer spirit to come into this area in 1918. Our Dad saw this Peace Country grow from its infancy—from no roads to paved roads and no electricity to power. He helped many new settlers when they came to settle here. He had a well-equipped blacksmith shop for that time. Some of the other settlers used it or he would help them.

Towards the end of his life, I asked him if he was "ready to go." His answer was; "Salvation is simple!" I knew what he meant by that comment—he understood what God's salvation was.

Mom worked alongside him. She came here as a school teacher. She and I became close during the time I was sick. My last visit at the lodge was the day before she passed away.

At the time of this writing, we have been blessed with two sons and their spouses, three daughters and their spouses, seven granddaughters, four grandsons, one great-granddaughter Calleigh and one great-grandson Carson.

We have also been blessed in so many other ways and hope that somehow we have been a blessing to others.

Uncle George was up visiting our family one time. He went out to Calais to pick up the Hudson Bay manager and his wife (Mr. and Mrs. McMillan) for supper. George took me with him and told me to sit in the driver's seat. I could barely see over the dashboard. Then he proceeded to light up a cigarette for me. I thought I had the world by the tail. But the object of this was to get me sick so I wouldn't smoke. I was five or six then, but that was just the start of things until I was 17.

Uncle Bill and Aunt Viney were mindful of our Christmas up here by sending gifts. One year Dad made toy trucks from wood, with wheels that turned, for us boys. I am sure he spent many hours on these to give us hours of pleasure. Probably we got the least presents that year but it was one of the better. I have always enjoyed visiting with Bill and Viney and the many discussions we have had.

Uncle Art inspired me in hunting. It was with him that I shot my first moose. We had many good hunting trips together. I got a guide's license one year but it interfered with farming so I let it go after the season.

Uncle Ed lived with our parents for a period of time when his parents went to Denmark. He was like a big brother to us. The day May Joy and I were married, he came down to my bedroom in the morning and sand in Danish, "When I was single, my pockets did jingle, I wish I were single again." Ed gave Norman and I priceless entertainment when he cleaned the dugout with a horse and would slip. He'd loosen a rubber boot in the mud and the lines from the horse would slip over his head and pull his hat off—this was repeated several times. Finally our entertainment got too much for him and he sent us home. Entertainment in those days was in short supply.

Short History of the Hennig's bv Alice (Adolphson) Henniq

Ken and I were married on Oct. 13, 1962. Ken was the Chief Ranger with the Alberta Forest Services and stationed in Valleyview, I was working for the Alberta Government Telephones prior to our son, Blaine arriving on November 29, 1963. Bonalin was a welcomed little sister at 5 months old and joined us on January 31, 1968. She was born August 30, 1967. In the meantime, we had moved to Grand Prairie, January 1965.

As I was a "stay at home mom" and our first dog, Sachemo, was a poodle, I reluctantly wound up in the dog clipping business. Also at that time, I took up golfing once a week and playing bridge every two weeks. Ken was now employed in management with Proctor and Gamble.

This life all came to a sudden end as Ken was no longer with P & G and we had purchased a "drive-in" restaurant in Valleyview in the spring of 1977. We had no idea how much effort this business required of us. We were both nearly dead after one week!!! Both Blaine (14) and Bonalin (10) were very good at working with the public (and loved the menu). It allowed for extra spending money for them when we all went to Hawaii while the business shut down during the Christmas holidays and two weeks beyond. We have some great memories of this short period in our lives. After we sold the "drive-in", I obtained my real estate license and Ken and Blaine had started up an oilfield sump treating business. Blaine later sold his share to his Dad, then purchased a Kenworth truck, and hauled logs in the Grande Prairie area.

In 1989, Blaine and Fawn had holidayed in B. C. after Ken and I had told them of stories of Nanaimo and that we would like to retire there someday. Therefore, they went there to check it out. They loved it too and moved there shortly after giving notice at their apartment in Grande Prairie.

In 1991, after the real estate firm that I was with closed its doors and Ken had sold the sump treating business, we were free to explore other ideas. Ken was working part-time for the forestry and I was doing a bit of golfing and curling and working on our new home with Mom as our new neighbor when Blaine sent an ad for a ladies wear shop that was for sale in Parksville, B. C.—just 20 minutes north of where he lived. It looked quite promising and after scrutiny by all of us, we purchased it. (To date, twenty years later, we still own it).

Ken kept working in the summer with the forestry in Valleyview and since Bonalin joined me a couple of months later, our family was all here . . . at least in the winter. Ken's part-time work mixed with a couple of years of full-time lasted for nearly nine years. Ken retired in the fall of 1999.

When Ken retired, he and Blaine spent many hours fixing, building and repairing on an acreage Blaine had purchased about two years before.

Then came the day our lives were changed forever Blain suddenly lost his life while hauling logs off the mountains on May 9, 2000 . . . on his dad's birthday. He was 36 years old. Blaine, after much searching, had met the love of his life, Diana. She is a lovely lady who still lives in Fresno.

He also left us his adorable black lab, Cinder. She died January 2005. To date, which is ten years later, Diana and Bonalin, Ken and I are in frequent contact with each other as we are with some of Blaine's best friends and neighbors.

Bonalin married Wayne Clearwater on a beautiful day by the ocean on May 22, 2004 and we now have a wonderful little four and a half year old grandson, Logan Blaine. They live in Parksville.

After Blaine's accident, Ken went back to consulting in the oil patch for about two years. He is now fully retired . . . . well sort of . . . . he's doing yard work, painting, etc. and walking Velvet, his chocolate lab, three times a day. However, he does take a couple months in the summers by going to his cabin on an acreage near Debolt. Using that as his base, he and his dog travel in the company of friends and relatives to the Yukon, N.W.T. or Alaska. I have joined them on a couple of trips north but I usually like to spend the summers at home, as the koi pond and yard are at their peak and the weather is at its best.

Blaine Kenon Hennig (b. November 29. 1963)

Blaine always dressed neatly and kept his vehicles very clean and well-serviced. He is a perfectionist! He was a bit if a tease, especially with his sister, Bonalin, but she could handle him and took it well. Sometimes she just handed it right back to him.

Blaine and Bonalin would come down to the farm and play with our litter of St. Bernard pups.

One time in the late 1970s, we went skiing in Jasper with Ken and Alice and their children. Whenever we stopped to eat, Blaine and Bonalin would always order a hamburger deluxe. Ken and Alice owned the Burger Baron in Valleyview at that time and Blaine and Bonalin could not get enough hamburgers!

The last time Blaine visited us, we had Sonia and Richard's boys at our place. He got such a kick out of lying down on the lawn and playing with them, and we heard a steady giggling. They played for at least an hour and then Blaine left for a short while, returning with some treats for the boys, and he continued playing with them. Blaine really liked little kids.

Blaine drove large trucks most of his adult working life, which included gravel trucks and oilfield trucks for Kakwa Haulers. This company was owned by his Uncles Doug and Don Hennig in Grande Prairie. He also owned his own truck.

He was the first one of his family to move to Parksville, British Columbia. He got a job driving these huge trucks that would haul large logs off mountainsides in that area. He did this for several years without incident. On his last trip down the mountain road with a fully loaded truck, he lost his brakes, went off the road and lost his life. We all miss him dearly!

Blaine had an interest in rodeo and made friends with cowboys on the rodeo circuit, including those of this area. He attended the Canadian Rodeo Finals and the National Finals in the U. S.

Blaine died May 9, 2000, and is buried in Parksville, B. C.

Bonalin Kay (Hennig) Clearwater (b. Aug. 30. 1967)

Bonalin grew up in Valleyview and worked as a waitress before she moved with her parents to Parksville. She submitted the name of her grandfather, Oscar Adolphson, for the name of the primary school, and it was chosen. When she was growing up she was an avid fan of the Edmonton Oilers. She knew the names of the players and their stats.

She married Wayne Clearwater (b. August 18, 1950 in Ontario) and they have one son, Logan Blaine (b. March 22, 2006). Wayne drives large trucks long distances in Canada and the U.S. and gets time off to be with his family on a regular basis. Bonalin is a homemaker and lives in Parksville with her family.

Ken & Alice Hennig visiting at Norm and Yutta's rented cabin at Parksville B.C. 2008

Ken, Velvet, Yutta & Alice Hennig (Adolphson) at cabin

Ken, Yutta & Alice on the front lawn overlooking the Pacific Ocean near the fish processer and ferry terminal

Picture taken at Alice and Ken's home at Parksville, B.C. after Blaine's funeral

Bonalin & Wayne Clearwater and Logan. Bonalin is Alice & Ken's daughter. They reside in Parksville

Grandma Ellen & Blaine

Augus, Janet and Cerian Macinnes. Augus & Janet
reside in St. Albert Ab. Augus is in Commercial assor
and realater. Janet is a registered nurse works for
Workmen's Compsation Board

Terry & April Barcesco. They live at 16700 Oaks Lane, Justin Texas 76247

Mia, Gabrelle and Amelia

Terry, Amelia Gabrelle, Mic and April

Megan & Chris

Janet & Angus

Megan & in her store

David & Cerian

Janet (Adolphson) MacInnes

Date of birth July 31, 1952 in Grande Prairie with given names of Hazel Janet and basic schooling in Valleyview and then on to nurses training in Edmonton.

In 1973, prior to my last year in nurse's training, I married Doug Bancesco. Following graduation I worked for a year at my training hospital, the Royal Alexandra. We built on an acreage near Onoway, moved there and had our first child, Terrill in 1976. Prior to our daughter Megan's birth in 1981, I worked for a family physician at the Weinlos Clinic in Edmonton.

Our marriage failed and I moved back to Valleyview for 2 years (1984 to 1986) while I regained my nursing registration and worked for the Valleyview Recreation Department.

The three of us moved to St. Albert in 1986 for a six month temporary nursing position in Home Care at Morinville Health Unit. The position became permanent and I spent the next five years as a Home Care nurse. I was initially concerned that my French was minimal and rusty, knowing that I would be working with mainly elderly rural clients who would not speak English. My patients were primarily French speaking, but my lack of skill with the French language was no problem. Communication became non verbal and there usually were children or grandchildren nearby to help. It was a job I really enjoyed.

I was remarried to Hal Haynes in 1988 for about four years. During that time I began working at Dickensfield Long Term Care for five years until my position was lost to Premier Ralph Klein's budget cuts. It was a blessing in disguise because it allowed me to attend NAIT for two years attaining a business diploma.

Following NAIT, I obtained a job with Alberta Blue Cross in the Provider Audit Department. This made use of my nursing background and my business training.

After two years with ABC, I began working for Canada Pension Plan Disability with the Federal government as a medical adjudicator where I remain. This is a job I find interesting and challenging. I enjoy the analytic aspect and the contact with clients.

All the while, two kids were growing up. We had fun and challenges and made a lot of good memories.

In 1997, Terrill Edward married his beautiful redhead, April Daugherty. He met her in Valleyview when he came up north to work for his cousin Dean in the oilfield. Her family has had close ties with our family for many years. Terry and April initially lived in Valleyview where he worked in small engine repair and for the Town of Valleyview in waste management. Terry and April now live in Justin, Texas and have given me three little granddaughters: Gabrielle, born June 25, 2001; Mia born August 28, 2002; Amelia, born May 23, 2008. In Texas, Terry initially worked for Wal-Mart as a supervisor and then area manager in their warehouse. Since then he has done renovations with a partner, done real estate appraisals and now works for Staples warehouse as a supervisor. April maintains their home, is a renowned cook and cares for two neighborhood children on a regular basis.

Megan Katrine completed her business degree at the University of Alberta, did some traveling and then opened a store in Sherwood Park in December 2008. Her store is called *mbellish* offering women's clothing, jewelry and gift items—all things she loves. The venture has been a lot of work and has developed talents she didn't realize she had. Her boyfriend Chris Dennis does commercial and residential renovations and they reside in downtown Edmonton.

In March 1999, Angus MacInnes came to Canada from Scotland in fulfillment of a lifelong dream. We met at an evening course at our church, were friends for a couple of years and then married on February 8, 2003.

Angus was initially a real estate agent but then trained as a real estate appraiser. He found a business that takes him from city to country and he greatly enjoys it.

Angus' daughter Cerian lives in Inverness Scotland. On March 17, 2012, she will marry David Baldwin. Both Cerian and David have degrees in town planning and met through their work. Cerian has done a lot of traveling and has recently trained as a counselor. She now works part time for the Scottish Environmental Agency and part time in her own counseling practice.

I continue to work for Canada Pension Plan Disability as a medical adjudicator. Angus and I do a little traveling when we are able—mostly between Scotland and Texas.

There have been many ups and downs in my life but I have great kids and grand kids, a great family and wonderful friends. I have memories that I would not have missed through it all. If life had been uneventful I might not have my faith and for that I am eternally grateful.

Index